Utopia

Key Concepts in Political Theory

Utopia

Mark Stephen Jendrysik

polity

First published in 2020 by Polity Press

Polity Press
65 Bridge Street
Cambridge CB2 1UR, UK

Polity Press
101 Station Landing
Suite 300
Medford, MA 02155, USA

ISBN-13: 978-1-5095-3492-0
ISBN-13: 978-1-5095-3493-7 (pb)

A catalogue record for this book is available from the British Library.

Library of Congress Cataloging-in-Publication Data
Names: Jendrysik, Mark Stephen, author.
Title: Utopia / Mark Stephen Jendrysik.
Description: Cambridge, UK ; Medford, MA : Polity, 2020. | Series: Key concepts in political theory | Includes bibliographical references and index. | Summary: "Mark Jendrysik examines the multifarious ways utopians have posed the question of how humans might realize truly human values"-- Provided by publisher.
Identifiers: LCCN 2019033282 (print) | LCCN 2019033283 (ebook) | ISBN 9781509534920 (hardback) | ISBN 9781509534937 (paperback) | ISBN 9781509534944 (epub)
Subjects: LCSH: Utopias.
Classification: LCC HX806 .J364 2020 (print) | LCC HX806 (ebook) | DDC 335/.02--dc23
LC record available at https://lccn.loc.gov/2019033282
LC ebook record available at https://lccn.loc.gov/2019033283

Typeset in 10.5 on 12pt Sabon
by Fakenham Prepress Solutions, Fakenham, Norfolk NR21 8NL
Printed and bound in Great Britain by CPI Group (UK) Ltd, Croydon

For further information on Polity, visit our website: politybooks.com

Contents

Acknowledgments

The roots of this book go back a very long way. My father, Stephen Jendrysik, the longtime president of the Edward Bellamy Memorial Association, first introduced me to the life and work of our hometown utopian. Isaac Asimov encouraged my utopian hopes and dreams when I met him soon after my tenth birthday. I would like to thank my colleagues from the Society for Utopian Studies. I have shared many interesting and enlightening discussions over the last fifteen years with Lyman Tower Sargent, Gregory Claeys, Alex MacDonald, Naomi Jacobs and Claire Curtis. Most of what makes up this book was presented at the society's conferences. My colleague and friend Ted Pedeleski took the time to read several drafts of the book and provided valuable feedback. The insights of three anonymous reviewers and the editors from Polity, George Owers and Julia Davies, improved the book immeasurably. Students in my classes on utopian thought at the University of Virginia, Bucknell University, the University of Mississippi and the University of North Dakota provided insights that inform every page. And, as ever, Kiara Kraus-Parr inspired me to do my best.

Introduction

Books addressing utopia and utopian political thought often start with a well-known quote from Oscar Wilde: "A map of the world that does not include Utopia is not even worth glancing at, for it leaves out the one country at which Humanity is always landing. And when Humanity lands there, it looks out, and, seeing a better country, sets sail." For Wilde, utopia is an aspiration that, once realized, requires us to seek for something better. There can be no end to this pursuit, this desire, this dream. But books about utopia also often start off with an epigram from Max Beerbohm: "So this is utopia ... I thought it was hell" (both quoted in Sargent 2010: 1). As a political idea utopia means liberation. But we must always ask: liberation from what? After all, one person's liberation can be another person's enslavement. And freedom for some has often required the oppression of others. One person's paradise could be another's prison.

Utopia has come to mean ideas that are ridiculed as "childish" or "naïve." Calling a political or economic proposal "utopian" marks it as foolish dreaming unworthy of consideration by serious people. In this light, the best epigram for this book is the famous statement by the rebellious French students of 1968: Demand the Impossible. Throughout history, utopian political theorists have proposed changes to the human social, economic and political order that seem impossible. And yet, many things deemed to be merely idle dreaming or radical speculation have come true. Utopian thought captures a longing, a desire, a hope, but also a need. Utopians transcend the limits of convention to discover the new, the better, the more just. They seek to "read the future into the present" (Beaumont 2004: 26–7). Of course, this desire has been perverted and twisted in ways that have led to oppression and death for millions of people. We should always remember that human beings have shown a tragic ability to create real-world anti-utopias or dystopias. The Nazi death camps, the Soviet gulag, "re-education" camps, the concentration camps for refugees that appear all over the world in even the most supposedly free countries, "reservations" and "reserves" for native peoples – the list is sadly endless. An honest examination of utopian thought must face that dystopian reality.

Any student who begins to study utopian political thought faces a daunting yet exciting task. Daunting because of the vast scope of the subject and its enormous and growing historical and philosophical range. Exciting because utopian thought calls forth a desire for a better world and presents the student with a massive menu of choices in terms of what and whom to study and where to place her energies.

Utopian dreaming expresses itself in many ways. Lyman Tower Sargent (1994) described literary works, intentional communities and social/political theory as the "three faces" of utopianism. This book focuses on the third face. But the reader should be aware that utopian political thinkers have traditionally used fiction as a means to advance their ideas. The canonical works of literature discussed here provided and continue to provide the foundation for the study of utopian thought.

Keep in mind that any discussion of utopian political thought will be idiosyncratic, reflecting a series of choices, some well-reasoned, some subjective and some, like utopia itself, inscrutable. Inevitably, works and thinkers that some consider important, even seminal, will be left out of this discussion. Students of utopia should be ready to accept a liberating uncertainty about just what constitutes utopian theory. Approach the subject with a light heart and an open mind and you will find utopia beckoning to you, calling on you to imagine the new and create new realities.

1
What is Utopia? What is Utopian Political Thought?

Defining utopia and utopian political thought presents a fundamental problem. When Thomas More invented the word "utopia" in 1516, he created a frustrating and fruitful sort of ambiguity. "Utopia" has a contested nature, because it means both "good place" (*eutopia*) and "no place" (*outupia*). Since More's original *Utopia*, all thinkers who follow in his footsteps face a set of serious questions. Is utopia a real place that can be attained by the efforts of human beings? Or is it someplace that will always be out of reach? Compounding this ambiguity, More's *Utopia* was not just a savage critique of the injustices of his times. Nor was it simply speculation about a state that, if made real, would create a just community. More's work was also a lighthearted entertainment for his friends. The book is full of puns, some good, some lame. The name of the castaway sailor who returns to report on the wonderful country of Utopia means "speaker of nonsense." There is a playfulness that lies at the heart of More's *Utopia*. If utopia is a desire or a dream, More reminds us to approach it with a light heart.

Homo utopicus: The Mindset of the Utopian Animal

Utopia begins with politics. Utopia might not end with politics, but the nature of political life, the distribution of power among individuals and in society, and the legitimacy of authority over the community lie at the heart of utopian thought.

We can begin with two propositions from the ancient Greek philosopher Aristotle. First, in his classic work *The Politics*, he declared that humans are "by nature a political animal" (1996: 13). If he is correct and we are political animals, then politics must be the central pivot of our lives. Politics is really the only thing that sets us apart from the animals. The organized struggle for power and authority conditions our lives and our societies. Second, if Aristotle is also correct that the good state is based on friendship (1996: 75), then politics becomes the art of working together and moving toward some realization of the common good. No state can be fully legitimate unless it is based on the actions of those who are equal, since true friendship is based in equality.

The political animal, then, is an autonomous individual who is able to think and act freely as a person. The political animal is not an individualist, valuing personal goals above all else. But the political animal is able to think and act and, most critically, decide whether or not to accept the values and goals of an existing society. Obviously, the extent of an individual's autonomy cannot be fixed. It will vary depending on many circumstances. But, to address honestly the central problem in utopian thought, the place of the individual in the perfected community, utopian thinkers must come to grips with the political animal.

Taming the dangerous and self-destructive tendencies of the political animal becomes the critical task of all forms of politics. Taming becomes even more important in utopia, since utopia strives for a kind of justice, order and societal well-being far beyond the somewhat ramshackle arrangements that have characterized most of human political history. Utopian thought demonstrates a revulsion against political forms arising from what the American constitutional framer Alexander Hamilton called "accident or force" (2003: 1). The utopian mindset questions everything, not simply to tear things down but to make us look at the world in new and exciting ways. The utopian asks how we can create a community in which authority, whether exercised by something we can recognize as a government or through social norms, is accepted as legitimate and good. So, utopian thought questions all social and political organization. As Plato said in his *Seventh Letter*, all existing states are "bad – nothing can cure their constitution but a miraculous reform assisted by good luck" (1973: 114). His contempt for the imperfect political systems of his own times led him to create a model for many future utopias, the community of total commitment, subsuming individual desire to the good of the whole.

Utopia is a humanistic enterprise. It is based in the belief that society can be understood by human beings and changed for the better. Any utopian theory worth discussing must recognize the value of our fellow beings and our moral relation to them. Recognizing a common good extending beyond the self, the family, or a particular religious or ethnic community remains the greatest and most utopian aspiration of all.

Defining Utopia/Utopianism

"Utopia" is a contested term for which "no fixed definition as such is attainable" (Claeys and Sargent 2017: 2). But in order make the systematic study of utopia and utopian thought possible, the term must be defined in a manageable way, keeping in mind there are exceptions to any rule. The idea of utopia is highly plastic and can be made to fit almost any political, economic or social system. It extends in all directions and can encompass any human endeavor. As Ernst Bloch said in his classic work on utopian theory *The Principle of Hope*, "so far does utopia extend, so vigorously does the raw material spread to all human activities, so essentially must every anthropology and science of the world contain it" (1986: 624). The danger here should be obvious: we can make utopia mean almost anything and attach utopian ideas to almost any human action. We must beware of a utopianism that is "watered down to the point that it can be found everywhere and nowhere" (Ingram 2016: xx). In that light, it is absolutely necessary to provide a rigorous definition of the concept to avoid confusion. However, creating an overly narrow definition risks removing much of the richness inherent in the study of utopia.

Utopianism might be described as a continuum. On one side, we see efforts at reform, exemplified by the "realistic utopia" advocated by the great philosopher of liberalism John Rawls (2001). At the other extreme, we find bold visions of the complete overhaul of society, first seen in Plato's (possibly) perfect community delineated in *Republic*. Gregory Claeys says utopia "generally represents ... a guided improvement in human behavior towards a substantially better condition, usually where society is considerably more equal and people are much better behaved" (2017: 265). The idea of a better, more just world seems to be a natural human aspiration. Utopianism is the desire to attain that better world here and soon, not in some distant future or after-death state.

In all its many forms, utopia critiques the existing order and, in doing so, "contributes to the open space of opposition" (Moylan 2014: 1). Utopia can be ambiguous, questioning its own very possibility. Utopian writers can demonstrate the dangerous potentials of utopia in dystopian works. Utopian ideas contribute to feminism and queer theory. Utopia may be found in small spaces outside of social norms, as in the heterotopia described by Michel Foucault.

Lyman Tower Sargent defines a utopia as:

> A non-existent society described in considerable detail and normally located in time and space. In standard usage utopia is used both as defined here as an equivalent for eutopia or a non-existent society described in considerable detail and normally located in time and space that the author intended a contemporaneous reader to view as considerably better than the society in which that reader lived. (2010: 6)

Ruth Levitas provides a definition that helps explain the place of utopia in political thought:

> The core of utopia is the desire for being otherwise, individually and collectively, subjectively and objectively. Its expressions explore and bring to debate the potential contents and contexts of human flourishing. It is thus better understood

as a method than a goal – a method elaborated … as the
Imaginary Reconstruction of Society. (2013: xi)

Utopia provides a platform to criticize our times and to
work toward something better. Any utopian work or theory
provides an alternative to present social, economic and political
organization. The "Imaginary Reconstruction of Society"
must be followed by efforts to really reconstruct society. It
is not enough to criticize; we must also provide answers to
our seemingly insurmountable problems. But simply reading
More's second book of *Utopia*, where he gives the reader a
report on the close to perfect society of the Utopians, without
reading the first book, where he delineates the injustice
and imperfection of England in his own times, misses the
point. The mixed critique at the heart of utopia remains its
critical feature, even when, in the present, dystopian speculations seem to have replaced utopia. Utopian dreams still
insinuate themselves into our current dystopias. As Lucy
Sargisson has noted, contemporary works mix "eutopian and
dystopian possibilities for the human race" (2012: 12).

Types of Utopia

Krishan Kumar suggests that four primary elements constitute
utopia. First, he says that utopia contains the "element of
desire," which he describes as an "escape from toil and
suffering." Second, utopia means "harmony." In utopia,
"everyone is at peace with himself and with other men."
Third, all utopias provide "hope." Utopia is the "promise
of a new dispensation" where "justice and freedom reign."
Finally, utopia is organized by self-conscious "design."
Kumar says that these four elements combine to give us "a
map of quite different possibilities for speculating on the
human condition" (1991: 18–19).

Kumar and Sargent, among others, link these elements to
several enduring features of utopian dreaming. All societies
seem to have Golden Age stories, tales of a time when people
lived in harmony with one another, with the gods (or God)
and with nature. But these stories inevitably delineate the

beginning of the current age of oppression and violence. The Garden of Eden is the most obvious such example, but similar stories can be found in the myths of the Greeks, Romans, Hindus and Chinese. During the so-called Age of Discovery, European explorers sought an earthly paradise in the "new world." Others in this period searched in Africa and Asia for the legendary kingdom of Prester John, a mighty Christian monarch who ruled a just state and would join with the kings of Europe to drive back the threat of Islam. Other traditions look to the lost immortal and enlightened realm of Shangri-La, the perfection of Atlantis, or the simple pastoral life of Arcadia. But not all utopians have such high aspirations. Some dreamed of a fleshly paradise or a "body utopia," often called Cockaygne, where food fell from the trees and work was banned. In such utopias, often identified with the dreams of the poor in medieval Europe, harmless license, gluttony and sexual freedom abounded. Finally, utopian dreaming can be seen in the longing for the end, the advent of the millennium. In the Christian tradition this has come to mean a time when true justice will be established. The dream of an end to the mundane world and the revelation of new and liberating truths crosses cultural boundaries. This desire has produced groups who withdraw from the world, such as the Essenes of the first century CE and today's religiously inspired intentional communities. It can be seen in the many forms of monasticism found around the world. But this dream has also produced nightmares in the form of groups such as the Fifth Monarchists of the sixteenth-century English Revolution, who believed the reign of Christ could be brought forward by violence. It has produced apocalyptic cults such as the followers of Jim Jones, who were driven to mass suicide at Jonestown, Guyana, in 1978.

Zygmunt Bauman points to nostalgia as a key feature of contemporary utopia. He says that "'retrotopias' are currently emerging: visions located in the lost/stolen/abandoned but undead past" (2017: 5). Such retrotopian ideas can be seen in political discourses that praise the "good old days" or the "greatest generation" and call for the restoration of traditional values (whatever they might be). The rise of ISIS, European neo-fascists, the American alt-right, or even

Donald Trump's promise to "make America great again" all show the power and danger of retrotopian ideas.

The ideal (but not necessarily perfect) city stands out as one of the defining characteristics of traditional utopian dreaming, planning and action. Plato's cities in *Republic* and *The Laws* and the actual experience of the ancient Greeks in civic design provide a template that inspires utopian thought to this day. Utopian ideal cities share a number of characteristics. First, the community will have a founder, an individual or group of committed people who receive the credit for the design of its institutions and its very existence. The greater distance in time from the founding to the present in a utopia, the stronger the power of the rules, norms and traditions left behind by the founder(s). The founder will have the kind of personal virtue that allows him or her to reconstruct a society on good principles. Perhaps this is why in utopian literature founders are often mythical or quasi-mythical figures. Second, an ideal city will be practically self-sufficient. This dream of a community that can provide all its needs and wants (which in utopia should be in balance, both for the whole society and for the individual) is rooted in the prejudices of ancient moralists who saw trade and commerce as corrupting. Third, the ideal city will resist change, since change is seen as decay. The Spartans were the object of admiration across ancient Greece, since their institutions seemed to have remained unchanged from time immemorial.

Claeys sees equality as central to utopia. Referencing More's *Utopia*, he says utopia seeks "to balance strife by privileging the communal, usually by making property and social classes more equal. ... Imagined or practiced humanely, it can teach us the enduring value of love, respect, the cultivation of the individual, even the eccentric and unique" (2011: 8). Making property common or giving all citizens in the community a moral claim on the products of earth and factory provides a common organizing feature of many utopian works. From More to Ursula K. Le Guin, utopian authors create methods of distribution and structures of work that allow all to contribute to the common good and take from the common store. But the equality at the heart of utopia is an equality not just of ownership but of duties as well. Utopia allows for no free riders.

But while equality is a key feature of many utopias, hierarchy and class structures provide another and contrasting feature. In early utopias such as Plato's, "we hear little or nothing about ... the great mass of people who attend to the economic and general life of the community" (Ferguson 1975: 64). Karl Popper says that Plato rests "the fate of the state with that of the ruling class; the exclusive interest of this class, and in its unity" (2013: 83). Many pre-modern utopians saw the need for a class of slaves or serfs to free the citizens from labor, allowing them to pursue a life of total commitment to the state. Orwell's caste system in *Nineteen Eighty-Four* is a grim echo of Plato's ideas.

Utopian thought looks toward a social, political and economic organization for humanity that is self-evidently right to the people who live under it. Utopia is aspiration, planning and action directed toward attaining a more just society. But an honest contemporary utopian will recognize the impossibility of a final answer. To avoid the clear dangers of utopian ideals enabling oppressive regimes, she will aim for utopias that recognize human autonomy and liberty and the dynamic nature of human society. Sargent sums up this approach: "most utopias aim to improve the human lot not by repression but by enhancement, and as long as we do not aim for perfection or eliminate the possibility of change, such utopias can stand up to the all-too-prevalent dystopias of the present" (2006: 15).

Defining Utopian Political Thought

Sargent says, "dissatisfaction is the beginning of utopianism" (2010: 48). But utopian thought must do more than just point out problems. Political thought that merely critiques existing injustices provides no way forward. Utopian thinkers must provide a meaningful set of ideas that might be applied to contemporary society. We should always keep in mind that many things that once seemed impossible are now commonplace. Utopia does not arise naturally. Its creation represents an act of human will that creates a break in history. Consider More's island of Utopia. The island was once a part of the mainland. It was severed from that connection by the order of King Utopus. What does this mean? Utopian thought and action require a separation from the mundane, from the existing world and its ways of life. Utopian thought seeks to open mental space for new and different understandings of how to organize our lives. In doing so it tries to expand the limits of what is possible and desirable by challenging political, social and economic structures that appear "natural." So, in *Agrarian Justice* (1797), Thomas Paine tries to change the minds of his contemporaries about the meanings of property, merit and desert. Karl Marx makes a similar effort, working to fundamentally shift understandings about the relations of labor and capital.

Utopian political and social thought expresses itself in many forms. In some cases, an author will present a highly detailed picture of a non-existent but desirable society, as in Plato's *Republic* or More's *Utopia*. In other cases, the principles of a radically different and substantially improved society are presented within a critique of the present and an explicit plan for political action, as seen in the *Communist Manifesto* (1848) or Milton Friedman's *Capitalism and Freedom* (1962). Situating utopian thought in this way, however, creates the danger of making pretty much every person who has ever advocated for political, economic and social change into a utopian theorist. Determining the difference between desire to reform or transform a society is a difficult task. Perhaps the best way to resolve this problem might be to consider various theorists in light of the questions and concerns that follow in this section. If a theorist addresses those questions and concerns with an eye toward what they understand as positive changes in the mindsets of individuals and in the ideas and institutions that support society, they might fit within the category of utopian thought. (Of course, since all such judgments are subjective, the final categorization of any particular thinker remains speculative.)

Utopian political thought might best be described as a series of questions. As Peter Stillman asks, "what conceptions of freedom, individual cultivation, and the moral or good life undergird a utopia?" (1990: 108). These basic questions naturally expand. We must ask, what is true human nature? What is true justice? What form of political and social organization will allow us to attain our shared goals? For example, how should property be distributed? How should the people be governed or govern themselves? What are the proper relations between men and women? How should children be raised and educated? How should a political community defend itself from internal and external threats? How should a society deal with social dysfunction and crime?

Utopian political and social thought embody efforts at creating or imagining a society that is substantially more just, more equal and more united (harmonious) than existing societies. The problem with such speculations is obvious. We must ask: justice and equality for whom? For example, Plato's *Republic* has an equal ruling class and subordinate classes that are excluded from equality and unity (although Plato claims all classes receive justice).

Ancient utopianism, such as Plato's, saw unity and equality as possible only among a small elite. Utopian thought in modern times, starting with Thomas More and moving forward to the present, has expanded the sphere of equality. However, this tendency has not ended disputes about just what equality should mean. The relationship between political, social and economic equality and the weight placed upon each make up key parts of modern utopian thought. The expansion of the sphere of equality is problematic because it works against unity. (It is manifestly harder to create unity in a large, diverse population.) Perhaps this explains why utopians from Plato to modern libertarians have seen utopian goals as obtainable only in small communities of shared beliefs.

If utopian thought seeks to establish freedom, we can also ask, freedom for whom? Freedom has been defined in many ways in utopian thought. For Plato and the ancient Greeks freedom meant the ability of the ruling elite to act as it saw fit. The concerns and desires of the great mass of people were immaterial. Thomas More and Gerrard Winstanley, among others, defined freedom as freedom from want and fear (expressed as having enough to eat and fulfilling work and security). Political freedom as we understand it – the ability to take part in communal decision making and actively consent to the actions of the state – was not of great importance to most classic utopian theorists. Even when they allow for elections and voting, as Edward Bellamy does in *Looking Backward* (1888), the self-evidently correct and successful principles of the existing society leave scant room for what we would consider political liberty. In light of this history, utopian thought now strives to establish what Erik Olin Wright calls "real freedom," where "people have actual capacities to make choices that matter to them" and "they have access to the basic resources needed for acting on their actual life plans" (2010: 18–19). In doing so, contemporary utopian thought wrestles with one of the paradoxes inherent in freedom. Establishing equality, and therefore freedom from fear and want, requires limitations on political and economic freedom. Establishing greater political and economic freedom seems to create more inequality and more fear and want.

All utopian dreamers have a theory of human nature at the foundation of their work. They may not explicitly state a theory, but an explanation of human nature will be there. Why? Because you cannot describe, prescribe or critique human social and political relations without some idea of what people are really like, or what people really *could* be like. Understanding what human beings desire and why they do the things they do are key tasks of any utopian theorist. Perhaps the most obvious human desire is to be able to act freely to achieve self-defined goals. This does not equal advocating socially destructive individualism. But utopian politics must recognize the individual and accept the individual's agency and value. Abstracting individuals into easily digestible and essentialized groups or symbols must be avoided. If "the citizens of utopia are grasped as a statistical population; there are no individuals any longer" (Jameson 2004: 39). It is all too easy to treat human beings as objects, as mere abstractions, to be moved about like pawns on a chessboard. Great reforms can be imagined more easily if we forget the human cost. It is much easier simply to express contempt and disdain for the "mob" or the "1 percent" than to face the claims of self-directing human beings on a fair and honest basis.

Utopian theory must also face the nature of political power and authority. Power must have purpose. Now, of course, the wielders of power might lie, both to themselves and the objects of their rule, about their real goals. But pure naked cynicism will fail. Those who wield or seek power must tell stories. They must provide a convincing narrative that supports their claims to authority. In the classic utopias this means a fully constructed story of community building, education and maintenance, as first seen in More's *Utopia*.

Utopian thought addresses political legitimacy. Authority can be defined as the use of power by particular individuals that is accepted as legitimate by the objects of that power. Because of the general aversion toward politics characteristic of utopian thought, the locus of power in utopia is often obscured or hidden. But any functioning and recognizably human society must have some authority, and that authority must be lodged in individuals, whether singly or in a group. Utopian theorists place the sources of legitimate political authority in various places. Some, such as Plato and More, or Charlotte Perkins Gilman in her classic feminist utopia *Herland* (1915), believe that the wise must rule. Aldous Huxley parodies this idea in *Brave New World* (1932), in which he makes his "World Controllers" suffering servants who are burdened with the knowledge of the dangerous truths that support their society. Bellamy makes individual political authority dependent on success in service to society expressed through labor. In Le Guin's *The Dispossessed* (1974), authority in an anarchist society comes from public esteem and respect for an individual's contributions to the common good.

Utopian thought presents a dynamic understanding and analysis of community. As social and political animals we create places where collectively we can pursue our goals (whether defined by the individual, the family, the community or the state). Community must be a place of both conscious and unconscious attachment. Members of any real and healthy community will be able to critically reflect on its values and compare them with those of other communities. Perhaps this sets that bar very high – after all, utopian communities in reality or in thought are often isolated from the rest of the world by distance or ideology. But mindless acceptance of the values of any community suggests those values are dead and fossilized.

Finally, utopian political thought engages and supports a particular idea of progress: the idea human beings can effect changes in the material conditions of their existence and that these changes are good. Utopian thought is fundamentally linked to technological advances that help cause social and economic change. Dystopia (or anti-utopia) appears as a live genre (and political form) when the dangerous effects of technology and expanding state power become evident. Why is this? Because technology allows ideologies to be realized. Changing the world to fit your beliefs is a lot easier when you have modern weapons and up-to-date tools of repression. But dystopia also reflects the fear that our political and social forms can regress and that old practices of oppression will reappear in new and more sinister guises. Commenting on the seemingly outlandish practices in *The Handmaid's Tale* (1985), Margaret Atwood said there was nothing new in Gilead's apparatus of repression, that everything in the book had occurred sometime in human history.

Utopia and Politics

Utopian thought is political. Utopian thought attempts to solve political, social and economic problems. Sometimes this can mean reaching toward an ideal state. Sometimes it can be tethered to current societal conditions and, "by showing how the social world may realize the features of a realistic Utopia, political philosophy provides a long-term goal of political endeavor, and in working toward it gives meaning to what we can do today" (Rawls 2001: 128). Utopian thought is not merely some sort of academic exercise. The great utopian thinkers were politically aware and active men and women. They often risked their lives, livelihoods and reputations to advance the dream of a better world.

Utopia is that part of political thought that sees beyond what is to what could be or, more importantly, what should be. While a realized utopia might seem to have transcended politics, the path to utopia, both in theory and in practice, must negotiate the realities of human interaction, of power and planning, of ruling and being ruled. As Jameson says:

"politics is always with us, and is always historical, always in the process of changing, of evolving, of disintegrating and deteriorating" (2004: 44).

But utopian thought can also be anti-political. Some utopian thinking is "based on a desire for the death of politics and the end of history" (Firth 2012: 14). Many utopian theorists sought and perhaps still seek what Thomas Hobbes called a "*Nunc stans*" – a final end point that renders politics, and perhaps even change, unnecessary. Utopia might begin with politics, but utopia seems to seek the end of politics. From Plato to Marx to Bellamy and beyond, utopian thought understands politics as an impediment to attaining justice and equality. A fully realized utopia renders politics unnecessary. As Alan Ryan says, "Plato's *Republic* and More's *Utopia* paint elaborate pictures of life in utopia but share with Marx the presumption that in the absence of conflicts of material interest, *administration* will be necessary, but *politics* will not" (2012: 771, original emphasis). Any examination of utopian political thought must address the clear tension between politics and anti-politics.

Jameson says that "utopia is either too political or not political enough." He claims that "in utopia politics is supposed to be over, along with History, Factionalism, parties, subgroups, special interests ... the one thing that cannot be challenged or changed is the system itself." But, and perhaps paradoxically, utopias often feature "eternal squabbling and bickering ... never ending debates and discussions ... interminable airing of differences" (2004: 42–3). Utopian thought is hyperpolitical and anti-political. This is not a particularly original observation, but it is one that should always be kept in mind. Le Guin's *The Dispossessed* focuses attention on this paradox. Anarres is at once anarchist and organized, lacking an "official" political structure but riven by power struggles. No space can be walled off and declared free of conflict. Unless a utopia is a benevolent dictatorship, such as Plato's Callipolis ("beautiful city") in *Republic*, or, like More's Utopia, it takes extreme measures to ensure that political debate is curtailed, there will be discussion and disagreement about its management. The expectation of most utopian authors seems to be that the inherent goodness of the community will be self-evident to its citizens. This will serve to limit contestation to relatively minor matters or technical questions of administration. But Jameson's main point is clearly correct: we should expect that utopian politics will narrow and become focused on administration while simultaneously insinuating itself into all aspects of life.

Whether political or anti-political, utopia must be plausible. Magical powers or the actions of benign aliens that lead to the creation of a perfected society belong to the realm of fantasy. Utopian plans may push the limits of the possible, but they must be real enough to be seen as plausible within their own context. Utopian thought and action are the products of actual human beings, not gods or superheroes.

Are Utopia and Utopian Political Thought Western Manifestations?

Kumar emphatically states that "the modern utopia – the modern western utopia invented in the Europe of the Renaissance – is the only utopia" (1987: 3). Sargent disagrees and claims that utopianism, defined as social dreaming, is a universal human phenomenon (1994: 19). Dreams of an earthly paradise, of places of plenty and of justice, appear across all cultures. A crucial difference between Western and non-Western visions of utopia, Sargent suggests, lies in the fact that non-Christian traditions lack the fundamental break represented by the Fall in the Garden of Eden and the idea that the Fall taints all humanity with original sin (2010: 68). In many ways, the debate over whether or not utopia and utopian political thought are products solely of the West turns on how one defines a set of terms. But what Sargent called "social dreaming," the "desire for a better way of being in the world," is universal (Dutton 2010: 250).

Recognizably utopian ideas can be seen in various forms of Chinese thought that stress the creation of harmonious societies. They can also be seen in anti-colonial liberation movements, particularly those of Gandhi in India, and in many African independence struggles, that sought new forms of social, economic and political life uninfluenced by the colonizing power. Some of these movements might be understood as retrotopian, since many of them stressed the restoration of a time before European imperialism disrupted traditional indigenous ways of life.

In this book I focus on Western thought about utopia. I do so for several reasons, the quality and persuasiveness of which the reader is free to judge for herself. First, the main development of utopian political thought has been in those places commonly identified with "the West." If students want to develop an understanding of the main tendencies of this tradition of inquiry and activism, they will need to examine its key exponents, from Plato to More to the present. Second, while utopian aspirations are universal, the systematic articulation of utopian political thought begins with Western sources. Third, I expect that the students who use this book will be concentrated mainly in the English-speaking world. An understanding of the ideas that are foundational to one's own context is absolutely necessary before trying to grasp the beliefs and dreams of people from other cultures. This statement should not be taken to mean that a student will judge other traditions solely in light of their own. It should be taken to mean that students will be better able to develop necessary critical tools and methods in an idiom that is familiar to them. They will then be able to move on to the much more challenging task of understanding ideas outside their own cultural context.

2
Utopianism Before *Utopia*

While Thomas More invented the term "utopia" in 1516, utopian dreaming and critique can be traced back to ancient times. Many of the elements of utopia are established in the myth/history of Sparta, in the works of Plato, and in the Bible. Plato's harmonious society and the militarized perfection of Sparta appealed to political theorists throughout history. Those who desire a final resolution of all political questions, the creation of new and just society, and guidance about how to reach that end have often turned to the Bible. From the Garden of Eden to the chilling visions of the Book of Revelation, the Bible has provided a fertile source of utopian and dystopian inspiration.

Utopian thought in the Western tradition can be traced back to the example and influence of Plato's Callipolis in *Republic* and to the myth (if not necessarily the reality) of Sparta. While Plato's city was ruled by philosophers, Sparta was ruled by its army. Every Spartan citizen was a full-time professional soldier. Sparta was admired and feared by the other Greek city-states. The small Spartan elite, which never numbered over ten thousand men, was dedicated to controlling a much larger population of non-citizens and slaves. The fierce discipline of the Spartans allowed them to be one of the leading powers in Greece from the seventh to the third centuries BCE. Sparta's stability and the dedication of its people to the state were generally contrasted with the democratic government and society of its great rival, Athens (see Cartledge 2003).

What is it about a thought experiment and a small city-state that resonates throughout so many works over so long a stretch of time? Krishan Kumar says that, "right up to the French Revolution and beyond, one way of classifying utopias was as "'Athenian' or 'Spartan', with Sparta predictably the favourite not simply for matching more closely the utopian preference for a tightly regulated communal order, but as much for its status as the putative model of the most admired ancient utopia, Plato's *Republic*" (1987: 5). So, "for over two and a half millennia politicians and philosophers, in the light of their own needs and convictions, have regarded one aspect and now another of Sparta as significant" (Rawson 1969: 1). In particular, "Spartan equality provided a vital precedent for Plato, More, Harrington, Rousseau, Robespierre, and many other later writers" (Claeys 2017: 11). As J. L. Talmon noted, the "myth of antiquity was the image of liberty equated with virtue. The citizen of Sparta ... was proudly free, yet a marvel of ascetic discipline. He was an equal member of the sovereign nation, and at the same time had no life or interests outside the collective tissue" (1985: 11). Sparta provides an example of the pervasive utopian dream of total commitment by citizens to the good of the community, and it was a key inspiration for the early modern utopias that reacted against the dangerous individualist tendencies of the Renaissance and Reformation. "The Spartan model suggested pre-eminently the qualities of asceticism, order, communal life and public duty." These ideals appealed to those who feared that the new ideas of individual self-creation could lead only to anarchy on both societal and personal levels (Kumar 1987: 36–7).

Plato's *Republic* has been a model for many utopias. As Kumar asks, "is it not a persuasive view, a commonplace even, that all utopias of the past two and half thousand years have been merely footnotes to Plato's *Republic*? What are Wells's Samurai, Huxley's Controllers, the Inner Party of Orwell's Oceania, but recognizable and legitimate descendants of Plato's Guardians? How frequently in later utopias do you not meet the characteristic features of the Platonic utopia?" (1987: 2). The desire for a society based on principles of reason and justice, and not on force, proves to be the most important feature of utopian dreaming for the next two thousand years.

A key part of the appeal of Plato's utopia and Sparta lies in their militarized aspects. Admiration for the apparent discipline and order of an army – the sense that military authority avoids distracting debate – helps explain why utopians return to the idea of a quasi-militarized organization of society again and again. As Jameson says, "the utopian tradition ... offers many kinds of examples of an attempt to project a future or at least a better social structure from the army as a collective institution, inevitably beginning with Plato's Republic (and with the image of Sparta that haunts the ancient world)" (2016: 29–30). This should not be taken to mean that utopian thought has equated society with the army or has advocated turning over all authority to soldiers. But utopian thought often sees that shared purpose and obedience to the common good inherent in a properly constituted army as something worth emulating.

Sparta as Utopian Myth/Model

A few qualifications are necessary before considering Sparta as a utopia. First, any statements about the people and society of Sparta can be contested. Second, the reality of Sparta is often in conflict with its mythic image. Any discussion of Sparta requires recognizing that the city-state was an outlier in the world of Greek *poli*. To the other Greeks, almost everything about it was strange and disturbing. Yet, Sparta, or at least an idealized vision of Sparta, held great appeal for many Greeks. Why was this? First, its (apparent) stability and the ancient roots of its institutions held a natural appeal in a society where change was always seen as decline (Ferguson 1975: 29). Second, "only at Sparta did the polis resemble a conscious work of art, in which everything had been designed to fix the thought and behavior of every individual in service to the community" (Dawson 1992: 28). Sparta saw itself and was seen by many outsiders as the only city that made "the development of moral excellence a public duty"

(Xenophon 1988: 177). The citizens subsumed themselves in the community and "viewed themselves absolutely as part of their country, rather than as individuals" (Plutarch 1988: 36).

In the ancient Greek mental universe, moral considerations outweighed economic or political factors in judging the success of a state. "Good Order" (*eutaxia* or *eunomia*) was a rallying cry for aristocrats, like Plato, who opposed democracy (Green 1990: 36–44). It appealed to philosophers who polished off the rough edges of politics and created perfected models of society. Good order meant a regime that acknowledged the natural inequality of humans and allowed the "best" people to rule. In this light, democracy, by definition, can never be good order. Plutarch says: "Sparta occupied the front rank in Greece for Good Order and reputation for some 500 years" (1988: 43). "Sparta regarded herself, and was regarded, as the embodiment of *eunomia*." The Spartans also were credited with the practice of *sophrosyne* – that is, prudence and moderation (Rawson 1969: 14, 20).

When Plato and Aristotle (along with many other lesser authors of the time) discuss the founding of an ideal city, they create separate castes of warriors and rulers who do not dilute their skills by pursuing a trade or farming. Societies of radical equality among a small citizen elite sustained by a large underclass appear repeatedly in utopian thought and in political reality. The unfreedom of the many makes the freedom of the few that much more valuable. The Spartan treatment of their large serf/slave class, the Helots, is only one extreme example. The Spartans literally declared war on the Helots each year so that a Spartan who killed a Helot would not be ritually impure. Spartan secret police forces systematically sought out and killed Helots deemed too intelligent or charismatic (Cartledge 2003). M. I. Finley says that, in Sparta, military force had "primarily a police function, aimed at an enemy within rather than at enemies real or potential without" (1975: 176). The subjection of the many allows the few to pursue higher goods – in Sparta, warfare, in Callipolis, philosophy. Sparta was a living example of a dream that has always mobilized elites of wealth or birth (or both): the permanent subordination of the masses to a self-selecting ruling class.

Lycurgus, the father of the Spartan state, stands as the classic example of a utopian founder. He is "a patron saint of the Utopian tradition" (Rawson 1969: 10). Solon of Athens and Lycurgus are the prototypes for lawgivers in several early modern utopias (Kumar 1987: 5). But Finley says that "anything referring to Lycurgus" is "almost wholly fictitious" (1975: 161). For purposes of my argument, the existence or non-existence of Lycurgus is immaterial. The Spartans treated him as real and ascribed all their best practices to him. Most importantly, he abolished money. This served, as it does in other utopias, to limit ambition, since money buys power and supports disruptive inequality. The end of money meant the end of disunity. Plutarch notes: "legal disputes disappeared along with coinage, since there was no longer greed nor want among them" (1988: 37). Lycurgus banned socially destructive forms of desire, replacing them with socially constructive forms that bound the community closer together. Lycurgus' laws "accustomed citizens to have no desire for a private life, nor knowledge of one, but rather like bees, always attached to the community, swarming together around their leader." Plutarch goes on to say that Lycurgus was unmatched by any philosopher and their "paper theories," since he created a state and "brought into the light of day ... a functioning constitution which is quite unmatched." He notes the Spartan theory of government was adopted by Plato, Diogenes and Zeno, among others (1988: 18–19, 37, 45).

Sparta's rejection of money and conspicuous consumption informs the utopian tradition. Utopian theory relies on a moral critique of wealth and money seeking. Economic analysis in utopian thought is never free from moral judgment. Utopia stands against luxury. Luxury can be defined in many ways, and these definitions always reflect the context and perceived needs of the community in question. One critical part of the utopian definition rests on the idea that luxury distracts people from their duties to the community and to each other. Anything that might cause a citizen to neglect his civic duties is defined as vice. The Spartans were blessedly free of such distractions. "No teacher of rhetoric trod Laconian soil, no begging seer, no pimp, no maker of gold or silver ornaments – because there was no coined money. Thus, gradually cut off from the things that animate and feed it, luxury atrophied of its own accord" (Plutarch 1988: 18).

In utopia, the true needs of the people replace false needs created by external forces. These true needs tend to be simpler and affirm the core values of the community. Luxury divides because not all can afford its goods. Necessity unites. Moderation limits social dysfunction. The "good order" at the heart of Spartan society was founded on the limits Spartans imposed on each other. They saw themselves as a community "whose inhabitants … possess neither too much nor too little" – one where "the largest number of citizens are willing to compete with each other in excellence without civil discord" (Plutarch 1988: 145, 157).

Spartan citizens referred to themselves and each other as "Equals" (*Homoioi*). True equality among citizens meant that the only real source of power was the esteem of your fellows. Sparta employed a fierce educational regime to prepare citizens for their assigned tasks and nothing more. Called the *agoge*, it was a comprehensive training regimen for Spartan boys that started at the age of seven. Full citizenship required successful completion of the *agoge* (Cartledge 2003). Plutarch says that the Spartans "would seek to be first in merit. There would be no distinction or inequality between individuals except for what censure of bad conduct and praise of good would determine" (1988: 16). Spartans lived in "fear of public opinion, which treated all disobedience and cowardice in particular so severely that life became notoriously not worth living" (Rawson 1969: 7). They needed "few laws," since their training in self-control made them unlikely to transgress. Complete communal solidarity enforced by norms, not laws, is a utopian commonplace from More's *Utopia* onward. Of course, there are often no laws in dystopias as well, for other, less appealing reasons.

To maintain good order the Spartans recognized no separation between the public and private lives of the Equals. The citizen body empowered itself to examine marriages, births, clothing and basically every aspect of life in the community. Communal dining perhaps best summarizes life under the continual observation of one's fellow citizens. Only Spartans who could contribute to the common mess were allowed to eat there and only those who could contribute were considered full citizens. During meals, respected leaders taught edifying lessons (Cartledge 2003). Communal dining appears throughout the utopian tradition, from More to Bellamy to Skinner to Callenbach. The shared public meal as a means of control and indoctrination seems to be an obvious practice given the absolute necessity of food for human life.

Any discussion of the Spartan utopia must address the place of Spartan women. It has become a commonplace to say that women in Sparta had more liberty than women in any other Greek city-state. But it is important to point out that the apparent freedom of Spartan women, their training in athletics, their life of discipline, was almost wholly in service of the eugenic goals of the state. The total power of the Spartan state inevitably spilled into matters of family and reproduction.

Plato's Republic: The Great Thought Experiment

Figuring out exactly what Plato was trying to do in *Republic* has kept generations of scholars busy. Was Plato really suggesting his Callipolis as a legitimate goal for our aspirations? At its heart, *Republic* takes certain premises, such as justice, the necessity for order and the nature of human potential and follows them to their ultimate conclusions. Those conclusions are not totally pleasant or appealing and raise serious questions about efforts directed toward creating an ideal community.

In *Republic*, Plato addresses several enduring utopian questions. First, what should be our true human aspirations? Mere life, mere physical comfort is not enough. We were not meant to live in a "city of pigs" (2000: 55). Instead, we must try to create a society based on true principles of justice. Second, who can take part in the utopian society? All utopian theories must face the question of citizenship. Third, what sort of education provides stability to utopia? Utopians who follow Plato see conditioning through education as assuring the foundations of the state. Finally, how should utopia face the problem of politics? Plato tries "to transcend the problems of conflict resolution with which ordinary politics must be concerned, and to build a society where total consensus can be assumed" (Dawson 1992: 75).

Plato's Callipolis arises out of a debate over the nature of justice. For Plato, justice is order. Every person doing what their nature intends them to do produces justice (2000: 138). If this is so, then the city must be designed to place each person in their proper place through eugenic selection and education. The city is built on a set of myths designed to create communal solidarity. The leaders of the city are empowered to create a mythology that supports the structures of the state. They begin with the famous "Noble Lie" (2000: 107–8). The rulers tell people of the city they are all brothers, born from the same earth. When they were made the creator placed different metals – gold, silver, bronze – in their souls. This myth supports the unity of the state while justifying what Plato saw as the inequality and class structure necessary in any stable human society. In Callipolis, the philosopher rulers with gold souls and the warriors with silver souls live in separation from the masses. In the best city the warriors are totally committed to war and the rulers are totally committed to ruling. The vast mass of people, the workers, with souls of bronze, are left to provide the services necessary to maintain the state. The principle of specialization, in which each person does the single task nature equips them to do, is the key to Platonic justice in *Republic*.

To sustain this idea of justice and allow all residents of Callipolis to work for common good, Plato abolishes private property for his "equals." He says the rulers and warriors will not "have any private property beyond what is absolutely essential." They will share all their possessions, allowing "no one to have the kind of house or storehouse which cannot be entered by anyone who feels like it." He concludes: "they should live a communal life, eating together like soldiers in a camp" (2000: 109–10). But Plato moves beyond these features to the even more radical step of abolishing the family. His ruling class is bred like cattle in order to produce superior people. Plato even refers to his ruling class and warrior class as a "herd." He says: "the best men should have sex with the best women as often as possible … we should bring up the children of the best, but not the children of our worst, if the quality of our herd is to be as high as we can make it." The rulers will destroy less than perfect offspring and transfer those who meet standards to the "nursing-pen," where they will be reared by professional nurses and nannies. Freed from the onerous task of child-rearing, the men and women (who have equal responsibilities) of the two upper classes can devote themselves to the state (Plato 2000: 157–8).

Eradicating self-interest is the key to creating total commitment to the community. Plato recognizes the divisive effects of family and private property on individual attachment to the common good. And so, "a fundamental objective of the beautiful city – [is] to sublimate or redirect all private desire, especially sexual desire, towards the well-being of the city" (Roochnik 2009:167). Callipolis demonstrates a "unity derived from the virtue and wisdom that bound together the ruling groups and flowed from there to the rest of society" (Wolin 2004: 58). The rulers and warriors share life in all aspects, leaving no place for selfishness or particular family loyalties. These features of shared property and shared lives are common across utopias and utopian thought. In utopian works "there is a presumption that with the abolition of monopolies of property and with the establishment of communism or commonalty the antagonistic spirit, the cause of evil, no longer would find significant expression in society" (Manuel 1996: 73).

By creating a class of warriors to defend the community and a class of philosophers to rule it, Plato also creates a great danger to the community. "Spirited" warriors often redirect their energies toward the domination of their fellow citizens. The warrior class must be educated to turn away from the desire to rule. They must be made excellent sheepdogs, content merely to guard the city, not rule it. The education system must also convince the rulers (the so-called philosopher kings) to take up the duty and burden of leadership, since they would prefer to stay safe in the realm of pure knowledge.

To achieve these goals, the city controls all information and education. Plato subscribes to the theory that children are blank slates whose early training determines their future conduct: "the young are incapable of judging what is allegory and what is not, and the opinions they form at that age tend to be ineradicable and unchangeable. For these reasons, perhaps, we should regard it as of the highest importance that the first things they hear should be improving stories, as beautiful as can be" (2000: 63–4). In the service of indoctrination, the rulers of Callipolis are empowered to censor myths and poetry, most importantly the works of Homer. All stories must teach positive lessons, instill loyalty to the common good, and prepare the warriors and the future rulers to sacrifice their lives for the city.

Plato provides some critical insight into the nature of the good state in Book Four of *Republic*. Disunity lies at the heart of every existing city. All types of government pit one part of society against the other in a sort of ongoing civil war. Due to division within them, they are "cities upon cities, but no city ... At the very least two, opposed to one another. A city of the poor and a city of the rich" (2000: 115). In such a city there can thus be no commitment to the common good. Destructive disunity and self-interest cause social and political upheaval, especially in democracies. For Plato, the "majority of people are not competent to care for and educate others in the deepest sense, and ... in democracy, freedom becomes so extensive that it leads to anarchy and lawlessness" (Fraistat 2015: 666). Callipolis provides an antidote to the disorder produced by all other political forms. Plato's best regime creates stability and ends the disruptive uncertainty that exists in every other political system. But the search for stability and permanence proves to be an illusion. The good city ultimately fails. Plato traces the inevitable decline from the best regime of Callipolis, through timocracy (the rule of soldiers), to oligarchy (the rule of the rich), to democracy (the rule of the poor), to, finally, tyranny (the rule of one). The state decays from the rule of the wise, who seek the good of all, to the rule of one, who seeks only his own good (2000: Book Eight).

Plato says that human beings cannot devise an enduring perfect society. But the ideal of the rule of the wise, the rule of people who are beyond mundane concerns, above personal ambition and focused only on the common good, proved to be a powerful one. The dream of an elite, able to see what is needed and unfettered by the petty demands of the selfish masses, arises again and again in utopian thought and human history. The belief that this elite earns its power through the sacrifices inherent in total commitment to the common good (as they define it) cannot help but appeal to those who see themselves as meant to rule.

Plato would revisit many of these same questions in his final work, *The Laws*. In it he seeks to create a legal and political structure for a newly founded city based on reason, not on force, since no state based on force can long endure (2016: 166). Here he expands civic education to the whole community, not just the ruling elite. Plato lays out detailed regulations for most every aspect of community life. *The Laws* focuses on the day-to-day lives of the citizens, covering in great depth issues such as marriage, hunting and public drunkenness. As such it is closer to the pattern of detailed regulation seen in later utopian works.

The Problem of Total Commitment

The Spartan experience and Plato's thought experiment reflect the enduring desire for communities of total commitment, societies in which men and women willingly sacrifice themselves, their property and their lives for the common good. These are communities where the citizens see their well-being as inextricably bound up with the well-being of the entire community. Fredric Jameson rightly points out that this should fill us with terror. Total commitment requires a "falling away of that imperious drive toward self-preservation" (2004: 51). In reality, an entire people cannot reasonably be expected to sacrifice everything to the state. So, ancient utopians and modern totalitarians fall back on the commitment of a minority that lives at the expense of the majority. This allows the elite to focus on the public good (as the elite understands it). But, in a particularly dangerous twist, the ideology of total commitment makes the people the continuous object of elite disappointment, denigration, contempt and ultimate debasement. It allows the ruling class to cease considering whole categories of human beings as "people."

While Sparta and Plato's Callipolis have inspired the utopian tradition, their approach is fundamentally at odds with any utopian project that recognizes the value and autonomy of the individual. Total commitment cannot allow for individual rights, since any deviation from the shared goals of the community seems like an attack on its very reason for being. So, politics must be degraded and ignored whenever possible. Societies of intense internal solidarity, of any size, see non-members as outside the bounds of law and morality. To us, such communities might seem to more dystopian than utopian.

The Bible as Utopian and Dystopian Inspiration

The Bible contains "images of the utopian past (Eden) and the utopian future (Heaven and Hell, the Second Coming of Christ, and the millennium)" (Sargent 2010: 86). These images have inspired utopian theories and revolutionary efforts to bring about the promises in the Bible. The idea of a violent and cataclysmic final end to all things often referred to as the Apocalypse shows the mix of utopian and dystopian messages that can be gleaned from its text.

Eden is a model of the golden age, a time of peace between man and nature, of innocence and plenty, before God cursed the Earth and condemned humanity to a lifetime of labor and suffering. Eden is also a source of ambivalence. We can search for it, dream about it, and even think we are near. But it always eludes us. And perhaps this might be a good thing. While some searched for the Earthly Paradise, others referred to the warning in the book of Genesis. "He [God] drove out the man; and at the east of the garden of Eden he placed the cherubim, and a sword flaming and turning to guard the way to the tree of life" (3: 23–4). To try to return to Eden or build an earthly paradise through human effort appears to be a sinful act of pride, worthy of punishment.

The desire for an end to strife and injustice calls forth aspirational prophecy. The Prophet Isaiah's vision of the lamb lying down with the lion (Isaiah 11: 6–9) and the dream of universal peace when men "shall beat their swords into plowshares, and their spears into pruning hooks; nation shall not lift up sword against nation, neither shall they learn war any more" (2: 4) has proved to be inspiration for peace-makers throughout history. Utopian political thought, while at times accepting the necessity of war, strives for peace. After all, as Edward Bellamy says in *Looking Backward*, poverty and oppression are the true enemies of humanity. The Bible supports, at least in some interpretations, the ideal of human equality. The division of society into rich and poor, noble and base, worthy and unworthy seems unjust. As the Lollard priest John Ball famously asked during the (English) Peasants' Revolt of 1381, "When Adam delved and Eve span, who was then the gentleman?" If we start from the position that all are equal under God, we are given a platform to demand equality in other parts of human society.

The Bible points to the end of time, the so-called millennium, when the existing human world will be swept away. For Christians, the Messiah will return and introduce a new golden age of justice that will last a thousand years. (There are a number of forms of Christian millennialism; in some the Messiah returns after the millennium.) Eden, or something like it, will be restored. In this age the good are rewarded and the evil punished. While institutional churches have always been ambivalent about millenarianism, the power of the idea has repeatedly motivated political action. As Kumar said, "the belief in the certainty of earthly salvation has transformed behavior, often on a revolutionary scale" (1991: 9). In the wake of the Protestant Reformation, the publication of the Bible in vernacular languages helped to fuel utopian demands. The Peasants' Revolt in Germany (1525) and radical political elements such as the Diggers, the Fifth Monarchists and the early Quakers during the English Revolution (1640–60) all employed the Bible to justify the total reorganization of society. In times of political upheaval or economic crisis people look for someone who will establish justice and order. Self-proclaimed messiahs have arisen many times in history. Some, such as Ann Lee (1736–84), the founder of the Shakers, established enduring communities. Others followed the path of John of Leiden (1509–36) and Jim Jones (1931–78), leading their followers to disaster.

The Book of Revelation has provided endless fodder for millennial speculation. The drama at its heart, a cosmic struggle between good and evil culminating in the victory of the righteous and the punishment of oppressors, appears in many forms throughout apocalyptic literature in the Jewish and Christian traditions. Revelation, and a number of similar works, provided the early Christians with guidebooks to the end times as they awaited the imminent Second Coming (Baumgartner 1999).

But, despite these examples, Christian leaders opposed efforts at re-establishing the Earthly Paradise or creating a perfectly just human society. In the fifth century CE, Saint Augustine condemned efforts to predict the time of the Second Coming (Baumgartner 1999: 44–5). In his classic work *The City of God*, Augustine denied that humans could attain perfection on earth. Original sin would forever prevent that. Augustine's rejection of individual human perfection expanded naturally to include the state. No human society could ever attain true justice. Efforts to create a perfect political community must end in failure. Augustine's position meant that utopian projects, such as Plato's Callipolis, were sinful in the Christian context. It is only with the rise of secular philosophies such as humanism that utopian thought became possible in the Christian West.

3
Inventing Utopia

From the standpoint of the twenty-first century it is difficult to understand the explosive effect of the discovery of the "new world" on the mindset of Europe. The new lands and peoples provided a template for intellectual speculation and millennial dreams. In *Utopia* (1516), Thomas More employs a classic form of speculative narrative, the traveler's tale, to lay out a nearly perfect society. In studied contrast to many explorers' narratives of the time, which emphasized the grotesque aspects of new lands (and were often simply fabrications), *Utopia* focuses on how human beings govern themselves. More says: "we made no inquiries ... about monsters which are the routine of travelers' tales. Scyllas, ravenous Celaenos, man-eating Lestrygonians and that sort of monstrosity you can hardly avoid, but to find governments wisely established and sensibly ruled is not so easy" (1989: 12). More's *Utopia* was first published in Latin, the language of scholarship at the time, and was not translated into English until 1551. The full title of the work on its first publication hints at More's goals. Translated from Latin, it reads *Concerning the Best State of a Commonwealth and the New Island of Utopia. A Truly Golden Handbook No Less Beneficial Than Entertaining* (Sargent 2010: 2).

In this same historical period, the beginnings of the Protestant Reformation challenged structures of church and state power that had existed for centuries. *Utopia* is also a reaction to that religious ferment. As Krishan Kumar noted, "the early modern utopia was an expression of the rational and critical spirit of the Renaissance and Reformation; but it was also a reaction against the individualism of those movements that threatened to tear society apart. It saw its function as the reintegration of society around a new moral and social order" (1987: 36). In *Utopia*, More tries to find answers to the crises of his time. Like all utopians he poses uncomfortable questions. He asks: "do we benefit from possessing ever more wealth while others starve; must states fight for prestige; can we tolerate religious dissenters?" (Ryan 2012: 318).

The life of Thomas More (1478–1535) was one of intense engagement in political, philosophical and religious controversy. Trained as a lawyer and drawn to the monastic life, More eventually rose to the highest positions in England. A staunch but not uncritical defender of Catholicism, his writings on religious topics on behalf of King Henry VIII won his master the title "Defender of the Faith." But More's life was filled with contradictions. He was an ascetic who lived off the bounty of a tyrant. A dedicated servant of his sovereign, he was executed for refusing to support Henry's break with the Catholic Church. A savage persecutor of Protestants, he defended religious toleration in his most famous work.

Even after 500 years More's *Utopia* remains the most influential work of utopian theory. One reason is that every part of this work is the subject of fundamental disagreements about how to read and understand it and about More's goals in writing it. A second reason is that More laid down the template for utopian thought as critique and plan. To understand his goals we need to consider the critique of his times that forms the first part of *Utopia*. Only then can the second part of the work, the design of the state of Utopia, be understood. There, More lays out the patterns that utopian works will follow for centuries to come (often pejoratively described as the "blueprint utopia"). Like many utopias that followed, *Utopia* is a work of "qualified optimism" in that More "locates utopia in contemporary semi-feudal society, rather than in either an agrarian paradise of long ago or a far-off tomorrow." Critically, he "expects *people*, not God, to establish utopia." And, perhaps most importantly, "More provides a detailed description of utopia, not merely a set of abstract principles, and his description reflects a close evaluation of his own society, not unanchored speculation" (Segal 2012: 48, original emphasis).

Ambiguity lies at the heart of this work and forces us to ask just how seriously we should take *Utopia*. After all, the book is filled with bad Latin and Greek puns. Utopia itself can mean "no place" or "good place." The name of the main river in the country translates to "waterless." The title held by the highest public officer in Utopia means "peopleless." More himself is a character in the dialogue, raising further questions about his position on the issues raised. Nevertheless, we should take More seriously. His passionate criticism of contemporary England and his meticulous design of Utopia suggest this work was meant as more than just a diversion for his clever friends. Like Plato, he seriously attempts to design a community that attains justice.

Utopia savagely critiques inequality and oppression. It attacks the compliancy of intellectuals in the face of tyranny. More asks his contemporary audience to reconsider the basic premises they hold regarding human social, economic and political order. He asks them to question what they believed to be the natural state of things – a world of scarcity, injustice, and harsh regimes of punishment. More's *Utopia* reflects a change in Western thought that should not be underestimated. Political and social change, once thought to be purely in the direction of decay, can now be seen as moving forward, toward what might be a more just world. More points toward a human world that has escaped the limits once imposed by nature, for good and for ill. He asks if our world and our relations to our fellow humans can be shaped and designed by conscious action. More anticipates that strain of modern political thought that rejects naturalistic or divine order explanations for existing or potential human political and social organization. But, as with everything in *Utopia*, it is wise to step back and ask if Thomas More, believing and committed Roman Catholic, endorsed the positions put forward by the characters in the book.

A time of intellectual, religious and political dislocation will produce many intellectual responses. More's *Utopia* was not a singular effort. Around this same time, a number of authors produced works we would recognize as utopian. Most notably among them were Tommaso Campanella's *City of the Sun* (1602) and Francis Bacon's *New Atlantis* (1627), both of which depict perfect communities located in newly discovered lands. Like *Utopia*, these works are presented as travelers' tales of societies based in reason, communal property and brotherhood. But More's commitment to a direct critique of his own times sets his work apart from other utopias of the era.

Utopia as Critique

Utopia begins as a dialogue between More, his friends and a traveler, Raphael Hythloday, who has spent many years in the new world. His last name translates into "expert in nonsense," but his first name is that of an angelic messenger and healer, providing yet more ambiguity about More's seriousness and intensions. The reader is left wondering how to reconcile Raphael, the "healer and guide," with Hythloday, "a speaker of witty nonsense" and retailer of what appears to be "yet another tall traveller's tale" (McCutcheon 1969: 38). (How closely Hythloday represents More's views is a matter of much scholarly speculation.) The voyager returning home with exotic tales of distant places is a fairly common trope in literature that critiques contemporary conditions. This becomes a regular feature of utopian works: a traveler is introduced to the life of the near-perfect community and is converted to its ways. Sometimes, the traveler returns to his home to share his experience with an often-skeptical audience.

In the first book of *Utopia*, More and his friends lament the inequality and violence that characterizes England. But, as products and beneficiaries of the current system, they are reticent to suggest radical changes. Only an outsider can do that. Hythloday declares that poverty produces disorder. He states that current conditions were not ordained by God but instead created by men. Changes in agriculture have driven the poor off the land, and efforts by the rich to enclose more and more common land for the raising of sheep has produced an upside-down world where the once docile animals "have become so greedy and fierce that they devour men themselves" (More 1989: 18). The now landless poor are driven to desperation by unfair taxes and the violence of a savage system of "justice." Hythloday points to the desire of princes for glory, leading to wars that kill and main thousands and leave discharged, penniless veterans roaming the kingdom, stealing to stay alive. In response to multiple crises the judicial system grows more and more cruel even as it becomes less effective. Finally, he notes that kings fundamentally misunderstand economics; they pile up wealth and impoverish their own people. A few enjoy luxury while millions suffer. Those who call themselves wise declare that nothing can be done, since misery is the natural state of humanity.

Hythloday claims that only fundamental changes in human social, political and economic relations can save us. Like Plato, he says that the abolition of private property is necessary to produce a just society: "I am wholly convinced that unless private property is entirely abolished, there can be no fair or just distribution of goods, nor can mankind be happily governed" (More 1989: 39). The response to this statement within the dialogue provides a classic objection to utopian thought. Hythloday's listeners automatically assume that common property will produce universal free riding. More's character asks: "how can there be plenty of commodities where every man stops working? If the hope of gain does not spur him on, won't he rely on others and become lazy?" (1989: 40). His answer delineates how Utopia trains its citizens to commit fully to the common good. He describes how the incentives that motivate that Utopians are fundamentally different from those that motivate More's Englishmen.

The Just Society

To understand Utopia as a society, we must understand More's idea of justice. He notes that, for many of his contemporaries, there are two kinds of justice, one for the people and one for nobility (1989: 87). The Utopians apply justice, by which they mean equal treatment of all citizens, to everyone in their community. While men and women are not treated equally (since More's views reflect the patriarchal beliefs of his times), the expectations for all Utopians are clear, and any distinctions between them are the product of reason, not accident.

Hythloday begins by describing the founding of Utopia. Like Sparta, the land of Utopia looks back on a semi-mythical founder. King Utopus conquered the people of Abraxa. He altered the physical and psychological landscape of his new land. As Hythloday relates, "after subduing the natives ... he promptly cut a channel fifteen miles wide where their land joined the continent ... He not only put the natives to work at this task, but all his own soldiers too, so that the vanquished would not think labour a disgrace." Like Alexander the Great and Julius Caesar, Utopus planned the cities of Utopia (More 1989: 43, 47). Utopus provided the Utopians with a ready-made state and an ideology. His triumph is so complete that the country takes his name. Utopus "brought [the land's] rude and uncouth inhabitants to such a high level of civilization that they now excel in that regard almost every other people" (1989: 43). His successors' only task is the preservation of his mighty achievement. From the conqueror's perspective this is a fantasy of perfect imperialism. But, in fact, "Utopia has its geographic and cultural origin in Abraxa's ruin, in its territorial 'cutting,' in its dominion, and in the forced labor of its inhabitants, commanded to build a new culture on the site of their own" (Boesky 1996: 20).

Hythloday describes the physical layout of the country and its government. The Utopians organize their cities to maximize stability. Each of the fifty-four cities on the island is self-sufficient in food since everyone shares in agricultural labor. Each city governs itself and sends delegates to a sort of national parliament to deal with larger issues (More 1989: 45–6). Utopia is a republic ruled not by the unrestrained desires of a king but by reason and the commitment of its citizens to the common good. Utopia "achieve[s] a society not governed by the contingent will of the prince but by a code of fair, public and preordained rules" (Ramiro Avilés 2003: 132).

All the organizational mechanisms of the Utopians would be useless without the abolition of "private business." "The whole island is like a single family," making the individual good and the public good one and the same. Only the end of private interest, embodied in private property and all the desires that arise from it, allows "every man to zealously pursue the public business." The Utopians have success-fully "torn up the seeds of ambition and faction at home" by removing their main causes, the desire for property and individual power. By keeping peace among themselves they "can never be overcome or even shaken by their envious neighbors" (More 1989: 61, 107, 110).

Wealth has no meaning among the Utopians. They don't value gold and famously use it for chamber pots or to chain slaves. As Hythloday says: "the Utopians are appalled at those people who practically worship a rich man." They understand that money has the power to warp reality, to make the stupid seem wise, the ugly seem beautiful (More 1989: 62–5). Their conception of honor differs radically from the aristocratic norms of More's England. The Utopians see hunting, one of the defining features of European aristocracy in More's time, as an activity fit only for slaves. The slaughter of animals debases those who do it, making them cruel. Though they fight wars to defend themselves and their allies, they find no glory in the so-called sport of kings, which they "despise as an activity fit only for beasts" (1989: 87). The Utopians see honor as service to the whole community, the protection of all its members, and not in self-aggrandizement. That is the reason we never learn the name of any individual Utopian except for the founder.

The universalization of labor provides a key aspect of Utopia as a nation and *Utopia* as work of political thought. Everyone in Utopia works; no one lives off the labor of others. Perhaps most importantly, no one escapes the hard labor of farm work. Utopians limit their needs. They dress simply but comfortably and reject luxury. Because they produce only the essential "commodities that nature really requires," they have more than enough of everything. The main job of state officials "is to manage matters so that no one sits around in idleness, and to make sure that everyone works hard at his trade." The Utopians are so efficient in their labor that the working day is a mere six hours (More 1989: 50–1). More's attitude toward labor, as an uplifting, unifying and socially positive act, becomes a key part of utopian thought. Unlike Plato, who regarded physical labor as morally degrading drudgery best done by slaves or by the disenfranchised masses, More dignifies labor as a necessary means of building a community of solidarity and equality.

This does not mean that Utopians live a dour life filled with self-mortification. Hythloday says that the Utopians seek pleasure, but the pleasures they seek are ones that improve the mind and body (More 1989: 53–4). They see the pursuit of physical pleasure as empty and leading to misery. The Utopians continually seek to improve their skills as workers and their minds as citizens. Public lectures are a favorite form of public entertainment, and many Utopians "spend their free time reading" (1989: 66). Utopia might be described as an intellectual's paradise, free from the base pleasures of mere sensual gratification.

Since the Utopians have "few laws," they rely on social norms and pressures. More believed "community pressure could be made to correspond to and to endorse conscience, and that the way to achieve this was though institutional and legal regulation, supervision and control" (Davis 1981: 58). The Utopians live, eat and work in public. Common meals are a key feature of Utopian education. Like Sparta, the citizens dine together, not just for the sake of efficiency but also as a means of social discipline. "While it is not forbidden to eat at home, no man does willingly because it is not thought proper" (More 1989: 58). They overcome the problem of free riding though education, surveillance and punishment. No Utopian can pursue purely individual goals. Conditioning, training and social pressures make it almost impossible for More's Utopians to do the wrong thing. They seem to lack the capacity to choose to do wrong. "If we mean by moral behavior a free choosing of the good rather than the bad ... the Utopian's area of choice is so limited that he is almost incapable of immoral behavior. In Utopia the bad alternative is, as far as possible, unavailable" (Davis 1981: 54).

But Hythloday says there are some Utopians who violate the norms and laws. Those who violate the few laws they have, which deal mostly with marriage and labor, are subjected to slavery. In Utopia, "the aim of punishment is to destroy vice and save men. The criminals are treated so that they necessarily become good, and they have the rest of their lives to atone for the wrong they have done." But behind this seeming magnanimity is a moral harshness created by a feeling of betrayal. Hythloday notes that the "Utopians ... deal more harshly with their own people than with others, feeling that their crimes are worse and deserve stricter punishment because ... they had an excellent education and the best of moral training, yet still couldn't be restrained from doing wrong" (More 1989: 24, 80). Crime attacks the social order. Punishment must restore a balance to that order. Repeat offenders are subjected to the death penalty. (For example, a second conviction for adultery results in death.) More condemns the overuse of the death penalty in contemporary England while opening up many opportunities for its use in Utopia. There is a moral calculus at work here that runs throughout utopian thought. It might be wrong to punish a man for stealing bread in England when he is hungry. But it will be correct to punish a man harshly for theft in Utopia since such an act reveals his essential depravity.

Religion and Politics in Utopia

The idea of a separation between church and state is a fairly recent innovation. In More's time, political leaders held to the belief that political stability required religious uniformity. Religious dissenters were usually seen as traitors. So it is remarkable that, in *Utopia*, More creates a state that not only practices religious toleration but also sees religious diversity as a good thing. Utopian religion is a "lived" one. Utopians practice their beliefs on a daily basis. They are more "Christian" than the so-called Christians in More's day. Hythloday repeatedly contrasts the brotherhood of the Utopians with the selfishness and hypocrisy of his European contemporaries. The Utopians claim toleration brings public peace and pleases God. Utopus "suspected that God perhaps likes various forms of worship and has therefore deliberately inspired different men with different views." While the Utopians are free to profess any religious ideas, they cannot be atheists. After all, "who can doubt that a man that has nothing to fear but the law, and no hope of life beyond the grave, will do everything he can to evade his country's laws" (More 1989: 97–8). Utopian religion might be described as a sort of polite monotheism, lacking much in the way of dogma, focused on reinforcing communal morality and norms. The hope that religious conflict can be avoided, if we just agree to disagree about particulars, recurs throughout utopian works.

Utopian organization reduces politics to administration. Local government revolves around making sure there are no shortages of food, people or labor in each city. National government exists to protect Utopia against outsiders. Since the Utopians agree on the goodness of equality and work and the desire to be kept safe, there is not much to argue about. Even so, any system of government invites the misuse of power for personal ends. The Utopian constitution is "based on the premise that the legal structure must restrain the natural inclination of men to seek and abuse power" (Cave 1991: 224). All office holders are selected for their prudence and are under constant surveillance, like all the inhabitants of Utopia, to prevent them from "conspiring together to alter the government and enslave the people." The citizens of Utopia "live in full view of all," without "chances for corruption; no hiding places, no spots for secret meetings." To seek authority by campaigning for office is a crime, and anyone who does is "disqualified for all of them" (More 1989: 40, 60, 84).

The Utopians, like their founder, are imperialists. When they conquer an enemy, they send their own people to manage the territory they have seized. These "Financial Factors" "live on the properties in great style and conduct themselves like magnates." They are quite willing and able to seize the lands of the peoples around them when they decide those "native peoples" are not employing those lands correctly. "The Utopians say it's perfectly justifiable to make war on people who leave their land idle." (This idea became a defining and justifying feature of European colonialism.) In another example of the perfect imperialism of the Utopians, the occupied peoples (at least those willing to live under Utopian law) happily accept Utopian rule and even become Utopians themselves. "Those natives who want to live with the Utopians are taken in. When such a merger occurs the two peoples gradually and easily blend together, sharing the same life and customs" (More 1989: 95, 56). It goes without saying that those customs are the superior ones of the Utopians. An important aspect of utopian political thought, and one that can be very dangerous, is the idea that a certain political ideology is so manifestly superior that all people should automatically recognize its superiority. Those who fail to do so are misguided or self-deluded and must, in the famous words of Jean-Jacques Rousseau, be "forced to be free."

More's Utopia as Political Thought

Certain aspects of Utopia might appear unappealing or oppressive to contemporary readers. People are transferred between cities to make up for shortfalls in population. While women fight in the Utopians' wars, the organization of society is resolutely patriarchal. The citizens of Utopia are under continual surveillance, whether by officials of the government, by their parents or by each other. Public and private life are not separated, and all individual actions are of interest to the community. But it is important to note that privacy, in the modern sense, did not exist in More's time. So, what to our eyes might seem like an invasive society would appear quite normal to More's contemporaries. But, as Gregory Claeys says, the price, the control and surveillance at the heart of Utopia "may be one many are unwilling to pay" (2011: 59).

Utopian thought aims at the liberation of humanity. But what form does that liberation take? We might ask whether More's Utopians are "free." As Hythloday says, "what can be greater riches than for a man to live joyfully and peacefully, free from all anxieties, and without worries about making a living" (More 1989: 107). More's Utopians are free from want. They know that they will never face famine. They are secure; their state protects them from the violence of the powerful and the criminal. They govern themselves and are not subject to the arbitrary will of some tyrant. They enjoy a bounded version of religious toleration. The liberty of Utopia as a nation secures the liberty of its citizens. However, the lives of the Utopians are constricted in many ways. They are conscripted for farm labor and can be shifted from town to town to keep the population properly distributed. They live under the patriarchal control of their fathers and are required to get the permission of local officials to travel.

More's utopians are not perfect. They fight wars, have criminals who must be punished, colonize the territory of foreign peoples, and are not above devious dealings with their neighbors. But they are not alienated or oppressed; they live in a true homeland, one that nurtures them and allows them to live fully human lives. They are "at home in the world" (Levitas 2013: 12). Utopian political thought works against alienation and tries to create a world that treats people as subjects, not simply as objects. In the land of Utopia everyone has a place and everyone is at home everywhere they go. The Utopians move about their land without fear, always knowing they will be welcomed by their fellow men. Perhaps this is the greatest utopian aspiration, to be treated as someone with value and to have that value recognized.

Hythloday suggests that the Utopians have overcome the critical problem of human life. Because they are able to produce all they need and more, they have ended greed. He says that fear produces greed. If people believe they will not have enough to live on, if they fear famine and want, they will become covetous, piling up goods against future shortages. Since shortages don't (and can't) occur in Utopia, human motivations have changed. The Utopians leave no place for the sin of pride, the desire to lord over others and to measure one's worth by others' misery. His statement is worth quoting at length.

> There is plenty of everything, and no reason to fear that anyone will claim more than he needs. Why would anyone be suspected of asking for more than is needed, when everyone knows there will never be any shortage? Fear of want, no doubt, makes every living creature greedy and avaricious, and man, besides, develops these qualities out of pride, which

glories in putting down others by a superfluous display of possessions. But this sort of vice has no place whatsoever in the Utopian way of life. (More 1989: 56–7)

Hythloday is on dangerous ground here. He seems to reject the Christian idea that original sin permanently affects human action. He says that changes to the material basis of human existence can fundamentally change human behavior (or allow true human nature to show itself). Since the Utopians are liberated from worry about their material conditions, they are free to pursue truly human values. This is a key and highly controversial utopian idea.

More, or at least his character in the dialogue, provides us with two useful final statements about Utopia and utopia. He says, first, "I was left thinking that quite a few of the laws and customs he [Hythloday] had described as existing among the Utopians were really absurd." But he finishes the book by admitting: "I freely confess that in the Utopian common-wealth there are many features that in our own societies I would like rather than expect to see" (1989: 110, 111). Any utopian society (or theory) will have institutions or practices that seem impossible, dangerous, naïve or simply ridiculous to the outsider. But, if we approach utopia and utopian thought with an open mind, some of those impossible things become desirable and, as we desire them, we work to make them real. The history of utopian political thought is about taking ideas for the reform and reconstruction of society and trying to make them happen. *Utopia* points to a new way of seeing the world, drawing on and going beyond old forms to create new possibilities. That is why we should take *Utopia*, and its author, seriously.

4
Utopia and the Age of Revolution

Revolutionary eras inspire utopian dreaming. In such times, fundamental changes to the social and political order appear to be within our grasp. The rupture that revolution represents opens space for radical speculation. The Puritan revolutionaries of sixteenth-century England hoped to usher in the rule of the "Saints." The founders of the United States proclaimed the establishment of a *Novus ordo seclorum* ("New order of the ages"). The leaders of the French Revolution instituted a new republican calendar starting with "Year One." The three great revolutions of early modern times, the English, the American and the French, each saw utopian thinkers put forward plans for the reconstruction of society.

Utopian Dreaming in the English Revolution

When the English Parliament deposed and executed Charles I in 1649, England's political leaders faced the difficult problem of designing a new political system. In the end, they failed at that task. But this period of uncertainty inspired a number of recognizably utopian constitutional plans and experiments. The ideas of the proto-communist agrarian reformer Gerrard Winstanley (1609–76) and the republican theorist and martyr James Harrington (1611–77) represent different forms of utopian aspiration.

The English Civil Wars produced violence and social upheaval across Britain and Ireland. The collapse of the old order created a fertile ground for dreams of the total reconstruction of political, economic and religious life. Millenarian dreams clashed with more earthly visions of what might constitute a just society. But, since there was no mental space for open, orderly political argument, all disagreement appeared as a sign of social dysfunction. So, any proposals for new political and religious forms required that dispute be ended and the common good or public interest be understood and shared by all.

Gerrard Winstanley and the Diggers

The Diggers sought to use communal experiments to show the people of England an alternative path to a just society by cultivating unused common lands outside of London in the years 1649–50. However, they soon came into conflict with local authorities and were dispersed. Gerrard Winstanley is generally recognized as their leader. In his final published work, *The Law of Freedom* (1652), he laid out a plan for a utopian communist community. Winstanley saw the current government of England as illegitimate. Its origin in the Norman Conquest (1066) and its continued existence were based solely on force. The people of England suffered under the "Norman Yoke," a set of cruel oppressions that stemmed from the system of property instituted at the time of the Conquest.

Winstanley created a new version of the Fall of Man. In *The Law of Freedom* he says that "Covetousness, ruling in the heart of Mankind, [made] one brother to covet a full possession of the Earth and a lordly rule over another brother, which he will have, or else inslave or kill his brother" (1941: 530). He believed that the present-day condition of humanity was a direct result of a sinful desire to possess more than a person needed to live. Covetousness was a product and expression of the Fall. The Fall repeated itself again and again as men sought wealth and power.

For Winstanley, the root of all evil lay in private property, in the buying and selling of land, the common possession of all humanity. Since the earth was originally given to all equally, how could it have been justly divided and handed over to a few? Force without right, what Winstanley calls "club law," created and sustains private property. Private property violates the natural law, what he calls the "Law of common Preservation." This law establishes our obligations to ourselves and our fellow man (Winstanley 1941: 529, 537). We can preserve our fellow human beings only when private property and the oppressive conditions that create and sustain it are abolished.

More's and Winstanley's utopias share a similar overriding goal, making sure people have enough to eat and enjoy personal security. Winstanley says: "True *Freedom* lies where a man receives his nourishment and preservation, and that is in the use of the earth" (1941: 519, original emphasis). Fear, the fear of not having enough to eat, and desire, the desire to lord over others, to take the products of their labor for one's own, are the roots of all evil. Winstanley's system provides people with all they need and educates them out of the desire to rule and exploit their fellow man. Like More, he assures his readers that the end of private property will not produce social disorder. Nor will universal idleness occur. Like More, he informs us that "there will be plenty of all Earthly Commodities, with less labor and trouble than now." When all work, peace is established, and men live in plenty (1941: 513).

Winstanley's ideal state, like More's, is concerned with all aspects of life and monitors all individuals. People are continually tempted to do wrong and must be trained in proper conduct. As Winstanley says, "Mankinde in the days of his youth, is like a young Colt, wanton and foolish, till he be broke by Education and correction" (1941: 576). All state officials, even down to fathers of families, are positively charged to watch, teach and punish. While there is no official church, ministers serve as information and propaganda officers. Education equips citizens to recognize that the natural state of human society is grounded in reason and equity (1941: 565).

The laws in Winstanley's Commonwealth are "few, short and pithy." They are easily understood, allowing every man to act as his own lawyer. They are read on a regular basis and all citizens are expected to be aware of them. Those who refuse to work or who steal from the common store are punished by slavery and then death. The law is designed "to Kill their pride and Unreasonableness, that they may become useful men in the Commonwealth" (Winstanley 1941: 597). As in More's Utopia, those who fail to conform are not just criminals, they are dangerous deviants who perversely reject the law and the common good.

Winstanley's ideas appear again and again in utopian thought. He bases his community on shared property, the revaluation of labor as necessary and positive, and the use of education to teach and enforce social norms. Perhaps this statement best summarizes his goals: "There shall be no tyrant kings, lords of manors, tithing priests, oppressing lawyers, exacting landlords, nor any such like pricking briar ... for the righteous law shall be the rule for everyone, and the judge of all men's actions" (Winstanley 1941: 535). A just state, like a good family, concerns itself with the well-being of all. But, as with More's Utopia, it remains an open question as to whether we would be willing to accept the limitations on individual liberty imposed by Winstanley's regime.

James Harrington's Immortal Commonwealth

In *The Commonwealth of Oceana* (1656), James Harrington calls for a revival of classical republican ideas to help create a society populated by independent citizens capable of total commitment to the common good. In Harrington's time, designing a republic larger than a city was utopian by definition, since anyone proposing such a form of government had to invent new words and new concepts. Harrington's goal for his utopian republic can be summed up in one word, stability. He calls his proposed state an "immortal commonwealth." He believes that good design can overcome the dangers posed by human nature and disruptive ambition. A stable political community relies on law, not on unpredictable human beings. "The liberty of a commonwealth consisteth in the empire [power and effectiveness] of her laws, the absence whereof would betray her unto the lusts of tyrants." Harrington famously says: "give us good orders and they will make us good men" (1992: 20, 64).

Harrington bases Oceana on the proper division of property. Property, in this case the ownership of land, provides the only means of independence for citizens. Independence means that a person does not rely on someone else for subsistence. Without landed property, no man can act in a manner befitting a citizen. It is impossible for someone in a state of dependence to exercise free choice. Such people – servants, children, women, the very poor – are outside the bounds of participation; they are literally external to the commonwealth.

Harrington recommends the implementation of a law called the "agrarian" to regulate landholding in Oceana. The agrarian law first divides the land and then restrains the accumulation of property. The equitable distribution of land defines a true commonwealth, a stable political community committed to the common good, since "a commonwealth that is internally equal hath no internal cause of commotion." Harrington says: "if the whole people be landlords, or hold the lands so divided among them ... the empire ... is a commonwealth" (1992: 158, 12).

The conduct of political life provides a second key feature of the immortal commonwealth. For Harrington, the main problem of government, "the whole mystery of the commonwealth ... lies only in dividing and choosing." He notes that this simple principle can be seen when "two silly girls" divide a cake (I cut, you choose) (1992: 22). Self-interest becomes the interest of all, because Harrington devises a system in which no one person or faction will both "cut" and "choose." It is in no one's interest to infringe on the freedom of others, since everyone will be armed with the means of (political) retaliation. Clearly, it will be in the interest of all parties to make the initial division, and all later divisions, as equal as possible. Under such an arrangement, reason becomes interest, and interest, reason.

What does this mean for the practical politics of Oceana? Harrington sums up politics as "dividing and choosing, in the language of a commonwealth ... debating and resolving." Therefore, it is necessary to create two chambers, one a senate for debating issues and presenting policy alternatives (cutting), the other an assembly for voting on the choices provided (choosing). The senate represents wisdom, "the light of mankind," while the assembly represents the "interest of the commonwealth" (Harrington 1992: 24). In Harrington's system, it is literally impossible for wisdom or interest, the few or the many, to infringe on the liberty of the other. "Harrington saw the adoption of his model as leading rapidly to the disappearance of parties and conflicting interests" (Davis 1981: 237). Civil peace follows the creation of the proper structures of governance. There will be little left to argue about, since wisdom and interest will become one. As in Plato's Callipolis or More's Utopia, administration replaces politics and reason guides the citizens on the correct path.

The American Revolution and Thomas Paine

Attributing utopian aspirations to the American Revolution may seem somewhat absurd. Certainly, most of its leaders were not radicals looking forward to a total reconstruction of society. Nor did they believe that political institutions could be means of molding and changing human nature. The founders of the United States did not expect to create a state based on total commitment or on the unanimous agreement of all people on the ways, means and goals of the community. They accepted social and political disagreement and division as a natural outgrowth of liberty. In *The Federalist* (1787), James Madison and Alexander Hamilton accept the inevitability of political conflict. In this way they represent "an American anti-utopian tradition that has persisted through many vicissitudes" (Gray 2007: 111). *The Federalist* challenges theories of civic virtue and the bad faith or self-delusion often present in aristocratic self-denial. Thus, Madison's recognition of the inevitability of faction and political competition in a (moderately) free society in *The Federalist* no. 10 can be seen as a classic anti-utopian statement.

But, in the midst of these "realistic" revolutionaries, one political thinker stands out as a potential utopian theorist. Thomas Paine (1737–1809) believed that revolutionary

America and France would provide bases for the liberation of humanity. In *Common Sense* (1776), *Rights of Man* (1791–2) and *The Age of Reason* (1794) he challenges the idols and shibboleths of his times: kingship, established religion, aristocratic hierarchy and unexamined tradition. His most apparently utopian work, *Agrarian Justice* (1797), reflects his belief that justice requires creating what we might recognize as the modern welfare state. In this work, Paine goes beyond suggesting reforms to demand fundamental changes in how citizens understand property rights and the causes of poverty.

Paine subscribes to a key tenet of utopian theory, the belief in the ability of human beings to shape their world. He sees human progress as inevitable, but he recognizes the need for direct action to motivate that progress. Revolution has not just effected political change, it has changed the conditions of human existence and the way we see the world (Paine 2000: 16, 30). Revolution frees our minds, allowing us to imagine new worlds. As Paine explains in his "Letter to Abbé Raynal" (1782), "our style and manner of thinking have undergone a revolution more extraordinary than the political revolution of the country. We see with other eyes; we hear with other ears; and think with other thoughts, than those we formerly used" (1969: II, 243).

In *Agrarian Justice*, Paine lays out the principles of a truly just state. He begins from a premise of radical equality: "It is wrong to say God made rich and poor, He made only male and female, and He gave them the earth for their inheritance" (2000: 323). Against those who claim that inequality is part of the natural order, Paine declares that poverty was and is a human creation and, as such, is amenable to human solutions (2000: 324). While the division of the world into private property has been a great boon for humanity in general, it has produced great injustice as well. "It has dispossessed more than half the inhabitants of every nation of their natural inheritance, without providing for them, as ought to have been done, an indemnification for that loss, and has thereby created a species of poverty and wretchedness that did not exist before" (2000: 326).

To right this historic wrong, Paine proposes a revolutionary system of social welfare. The benefits to be provided are a sort of reparation for the loss of property suffered by most of humanity. He says: "it is not charity but a right, not bounty but justice, that I am pleading for. The present state of civilization is as odious as it is unjust" (2000: 331). The centerpiece of Paine's plan is an award of £15 to each person who reaches the age of twenty-one, "as compensation, in part, for the loss of his or her natural inheritance, by the introduction of the system of landed property," and an old-age pension of £10 a year once an individual reaches the age of fifty. Justice requires that the state make this provision, since the charitable actions of private individuals are capricious and unpredictable. "In all great cases it is necessary to have a principle more universally active than charity; and with respect to justice, it ought not to be left to the choice of detached individuals whether they will do justice or not" (2000: 327, 332). Paine recognized that we cannot simply appeal to some universal sense of justice if we are successfully to implement such a project. Self-interest plays a role as well. Since the vast majority of people are poor, or at least not rich, they will benefit from the security provided by the plan. The wealthy will also benefit from reduced social upheaval and unrest. Finally, since humans do not create themselves and no person really generates his own wealth, all people have a mutual debt to every other person and to society. Paine's explanation of why this is the case is worth quoting in full:

> Separate an individual from society, and give him an island or a continent to possess, and he cannot acquire personal property. He cannot be rich. So inseparably are the means connected with the end, in all cases, that where the former do not exist the latter cannot be obtained. All accumulation, therefore, of personal property, beyond what a man's own hands produce, is derived to him by living in society; and he owes on every principle of justice, of gratitude, and of civilization, a part of that accumulation back again to society from whence the whole came. (2000: 334)

Paine had a boundless faith in the ability of ordinary human beings to shape their social, political and economic worlds. Human beings create their own futures, and they do so by acts of reason and free will. People truly have the power to begin the world all over again. They can sweep away the accreted injustices of the centuries and establish, if not an earthly Jerusalem, a just and equal society in which all people are free to attain their full potential. Paine's utopia, then, is not a place; it is a condition.

Jean-Jacques Rousseau and the French Revolution

A key difference between the French and American revolutions lies in the question of how to deal with disagreement over the common good. While the American founders were able to design a theory to accommodate differences of opinion, the French revolutionaries sought to establish a republic that would be one and indivisible, not just in terms of organization but also in belief. They created the idea of the nation-state, a new form of political organization justified in calling upon all its citizens to make sacrifices for the common good. As the revolutionary author Emmanuel Joseph Sieyès said in 1789, "the nation is prior to everything. It is the source of everything. Its will is always legal; indeed it is the law itself" (quoted in Schaer 2000: 191). This "imagined community" demands our loyalty, imposes obligations, and makes claims that supersede all others (Anderson 1991). The ubiquity of the nation-state in today's world obscures just how utopian (and perhaps even absurd) these claims would seem in the late eighteenth century.

While it is always dangerous to trace political actions back to the ideas of a single author, the influence of Jean-Jacques Rousseau (1712–78) on the French Revolution and on modern political thought cannot be overestimated. Was he a utopian? Plausible arguments can be made pro and con. Rousseau did not believe that human beings could create permanent or "immortal" political structures. In *The Social Contract* (1762), he says: "if Sparta and Rome perished, what State can hope to last forever?" (1997b: 109). We cannot prevent the inevitable decay of all human creations. But this does not mean we cannot redesign the world. Rousseau believed that human beings are corrupted not by original sin (in its Christian sense) but by social orders that create perverse incentives by continuously rewarding antisocial actions (1997a: 198). He thinks that we can change society, allowing it to become a vehicle to mold our natures into something positive. By doing so, we can discover the common interest of society and implement it. In this way, Rousseau "paved the way for the utopian optimism of Marxism and other radical political movements of the past two centuries" (Ryan 2012: 537).

Understanding Rousseau's contribution to utopian political thought requires examining his history of human nature and society presented in the *Discourse on the Origin of Inequality* (1755), in which he declares inequality unnatural and claims that equality is the norm for human society. He presents a secular version of the Fall, where the creation of private property produces dystopian effects. Before the imposition of private property on humanity, people lived in equality, and their instincts for their own preservation and the preservation of their fellows guided their actions. They lived a healthy life, both mentally and physically. They were not oppressed by desires they could never reach, nor did they live in fear of death. While some might consider this life to be a sort of utopia worth returning to, Rousseau clearly believes that we can never return to this primordial state because the creation of property irrevocably changed all human relations (1997a: 164ff.). He says:

> the first man who, having enclosed a piece of ground, to whom it occurred to say *this is mine*, and found people sufficiently simple to believe him, was the true founder of civil society. How many crimes, wars, murders, how many miseries and horrors Mankind would have been spared by him who, pulling up the stakes or filling in the ditch, had cried out to his kind: Beware of listening to this imposter. You are lost if you forget that the fruits are everyone's and the Earth is no one's. (1997a: 161, original emphasis)

Almost instantly "the vast forests changed into smiling fields that had to be watered with the sweat of men, and where slavery and misery were soon seen to sprout and grow together with the harvests" (1997a: 167). Private property resulted in a war of all against all as men enriched themselves and exploited their fellows. Faced with this anarchical situation, people "ran toward their chains in the belief they were securing their freedom" (1997a: 173). They created governments that reinforced the existing divisions of society and concentrated power and wealth in fewer and fewer hands. In this new and cruel state, "a handful of people abound in superfluities while the starving multitude lacks in necessities" (1997a: 188). The *Discourse* ends on a very dark note. Our desire to protect our property or our lives leads us to surrender our freedom for the illusion of security.

Rousseau delineates a potential means of escape from this dystopian situation in *The Social Contract*. Famously, he begins by saying that "man is born free, and everywhere he is in chains" (1997b: 41). To escape this situation, we must be "forced to be free," to identify our good with the good of our society (1997b: 53). To achieve this goal, Rousseau resurrects the Spartan dream of total commitment and total solidarity. Creating this society requires establishing what he calls "the General Will." While defining just what he means by this term is difficult, a good definition might be that "my will (any will) is general if and only if it has as its object that which is common to all concerned" (Strong 1994: 85). The General Will is an unerring expression of the true common good in any political community. It is indivisible, infallible and perfect. An individual's private good can only be attained in harmony with the public good.

To create this new order, a superhuman "Lawgiver" must arise. The Lawgiver must be "capable of, so to speak, changing human nature, of transforming each individual who by himself is a perfect and solitary whole into part of a larger whole from which the individual would as it were receive his life and his being" (Rousseau 1997b: 69). Like Lycurgus, the Lawgiver creates a new society. "The task of the legislator is to create a new type of man, with a new mentality, new values ... free from old instincts, prejudices and bad habits." Like all utopian founders, the Legislator relies less on law and more on the creation of a shared set of social norms to bind the community together. The good society follows the Spartan example, "where Lycurgus established morals that almost made the addition of Laws unnecessary" (1997a: 182). For its "genuine constitution," the best state will rely on "morals, customs, and above all opinion" until citizens obey from the heart and by habit, not out of fear of punishment (1997b: 81). The practical demonstration of the success of the Lawgiver and the implementation of the General Will is shown by the creation of a state with no factions, no "partial societies" (1997b: 60). All citizens mind the public business. Once they lose this commitment, the state is doomed. Rousseau states: "as soon as someone says about affairs of State *What do I care?* the State can be considered lost" (1997b: 114, original emphasis).

Rousseau did not believe this form of political organization could be applied to large political bodies. Only in the city-state could citizens develop the shared affection and consciousness necessary to truly govern themselves: "the more the social bond stretches the looser it grows, and in general a small State is stronger than a large one" (1997b: 74). Large political communities cannot attain the total commitment that characterizes the citizen in a city-state (1997b: 193ff.). In his *Considerations on the Government of Poland* (1772), Rousseau says that the best larger states can do is to try to educate citizens as patriots who will attach themselves to the well-being of the nation and overcome the selfishness that undermines the state (1997b: 192).

The Problem of Utopia and Revolution

What do all these revolutionary utopians have in common? They share the belief that people alive today can and must reshape the world. Paine and Rousseau believed human beings could create, through acts of will and the application of reason, a whole new world. But Paine's belief in the obvious rightness of his ideas has the same dangerous effect as Rousseau's dream of unity in a state that has molded the minds and hearts of men. In trying to create equality and establish justice, utopian thought succumbs to the trap of "forcing people to be free." This kind of utopian desire opens the door to violent social engineering by a revolutionary elite. The dream of unity makes opposition to the revolutionary powers a counter-revolutionary act. The belief that human beings are free to shape their world through acts of will is the key utopian idea. It is at once liberating and frightening. Because if we are free to make the world over, and make it better, we also have the power to make the world worse, and in that case we have no one to blame but ourselves.

5
Utopia and Modernity

Utopian political thought rose to its greatest prominence in the nineteenth century. Hundreds of works of utopian fiction, along with experiments in new forms of communal living, tested the limits of the possible, created political movements, and challenged the dominant paradigm of unfettered capitalism. In this era the promises and perils of technological change became evident. Long-established patterns of life and production were overturned. Millions migrated from farm to factory and across oceans. Economic growth marched hand in hand with growing inequality. The key revolutionary ideals of the eighteenth century, individual rights and expanded political participation, clashed with the old aristocratic and new capitalist defenders of privilege.

Varieties of Nineteenth- and Early Twentieth-Century Utopian Thought

Many experimental communities arose in the nineteenth century. Designed to moderate the effects of unregulated capitalism, or provide an escape from it, they were often short-lived, failing to survive the pressures of the larger society. But these communities, particularly those inspired by the work of Henri de Saint-Simon (1760–1825), Robert

Owen (1771–1858), Étienne Cabet (1788–1856), Charles Fourier (1772–1837) and John Humphrey Noyes (1813–86), provided a challenge, an alternative vision, against rampant, unrestrained capitalism. They are often described as "utopian socialists" to distinguish them from "scientific" socialists such as Karl Marx. However, as Vincent Geoghegan notes, "time and time again in their work they asserted the hard-headed, scientific, realistic and practical approach to society. There was nothing 'utopian', as they understood the term, in their methodology" (1987: 8). Keith Taylor echoes this assessment, saying: "They preferred to think of themselves as scientists rather than utopians, since they believed they had attained a truly objective understanding of the ways in which western societies were actually developing, and an equally objective insight into how they could be organised in future so as to maximise human happiness" (1982: 2).

The ideas of Owen and Fourier helped provide the foundations for British and French socialist thought (Claeys 2011: 132). Noyes's community in Oneida, New York, survived for thirty years after its founding in 1848. Owen's planned factory community at New Lanark in Scotland survived for several decades and provided "proof that capitalist principles could be reconciled with workers' wellbeing." Fourier's ideas inspired the formation of thirty communities in the United States, most notably Brook Farm, founded by the famous authors Ralph Waldo Emerson and Henry David Thoreau (ibid., 132, 135). Cabet established three communities in the United States based on the principles laid out in his utopian novel *Voyage in Icarie* (1840) (Kumar 1991: 70). While the communities established by Cabet and the disciples of Fourier lasted only a few years at most, like Oneida and New Lanark, they presented alternative forms of social and economic order. Their existence showed "the societies of tomorrow *in operation*, thus providing a fact-based image of possible realities" (Siméon 2017: 96, original emphasis). In Owen's words, such communities demonstrated "that these principles have been carried most successfully into practice" (2019: 21).

While it is dangerous to generalize about such a diverse group of thinkers, they held several common beliefs. They believed that human nature, or at least our perception of human nature, had been distorted by the pressures of society (see Owen 2019: 59; Fourier 1996: 23ff.), and they agreed that capitalism undermined human happiness and produced conflict that destroyed social harmony. In response, they saw the need for communities built on cooperative enterprises in all facets of life (Taylor 1982: 8–9). Like earlier utopians, they sought to replace politics, which they saw as a corrupt and corrupting struggle for power, with administration (Geoghegan 1987: 13). They rejected revolutionary action in favor of gradual processes of social change. The self-evident goodness of those changes and their positive effects would lead to their universal adaptation (Taylor 1982: 14–16). For Owen, "the truth of his principles would naturally gradually encourage mankind to relocate in a network of self-supporting communities, ultimately superseding all existing institutions and forms of government" (Siméon 2017: 2). In actual practice, these principles required the creation of communities where labor was valued and shared, where private property, if not abolished, was limited, and where the education of children was a communal enterprise. The communities they created or inspired used such classic utopian methods as common meals, shared labor and the physical design of the community to enforce cooperation and maintenance of communal norms (Claeys 2011: 132–7). The so-called utopian socialists represent a revival of older utopian ideas combined with the recognition of the necessity for new answers to the changes brought by capitalism.

In this period, utopian thought was also expressed in literature. The late nineteenth and early twentieth centuries represent the high point of popularity for the literary utopia. Edward Bellamy's *Looking Backward* (1888), William Morris's *News from Nowhere* (1890), H. G. Wells's *A Modern Utopia* (1905) and Charlotte Perkins Gilman's *Herland* (1915) are four of the most important works of this period. Like the so-called utopian socialists, these authors address, in different ways, the dislocations of capitalist modernity. They create utopias of abundance, arguing that human security and fulfillment does not mean self-denial. All reject the idea of original sin, believing that utopian organization reveals true human nature. They reflect and critique each other. Morris directly criticizes Bellamy's utopia, while

Wells critiques both their works. Gilman responds to the patriarchal assumptions that underlay the utopias of the era. *News from Nowhere* points the way to the ecological or green utopia, where people live in harmony with nature and limit their needs. Each of these works reflects its times. In them, these authors discuss and accept the ideas of eugenics popular at the time. They all describe the good health and "race improvement" brought about through utopian organization. But they show little to no interest in the question of race. Bellamy, Wells and Morris create utopias that seem to elevate the status of women but still relegate them mostly to the role of men's helpmate and domestic ornament.

All four of these authors were prolific writers, and it is vital not to assume that the positions they took in these canonical works represent their complete statements on the issues noted above. In *Equality* (1897), his sequel to *Looking Backward*, Bellamy makes women full and equal members of society. Wells would struggle with the place of women in society throughout his long career. He eventually rejected eugenics (Parrington 2003). Gilman published a number of works that were explicitly racist, and Bellamy took a number of contradictory positions on race (Robertson 2018: 74, 215ff.).

Bellamy's Disciplined Utopia

Edward Bellamy's *Looking Backward* describes the visit of a time traveler from the late nineteenth century to the city of Boston in the year 2000. Within two years the book sold half a million copies in the United States and over 200,000 in Britain (Robertson 2018: 38). Bellamy vigorously denied his ideas were "socialist," preferring to call his theories "Nationalism." In his ideal state, the nation would control the means of production and order society on a central plan. Bellamy clubs sprung up around the world, and he founded a series of newspapers to advance his theories. Nationalism enjoyed a period of public interest and political influence in radical circles in the United States in the 1890s (Kumar 1987: chap. 5). Bellamy's support for the public ownership of utilities had some successes in the northeastern United States and was embraced by in the 1930s by "New Deal intellectuals, most notably Arthur Morgan, who served as founding director of the Tennessee Valley Authority" (Robertson 2018: 76).

Looking Backward begins with a powerful critique of capitalism in the allegorical "Story of the Coach." Bellamy describes contemporary society as a coach being pulled along a rough and hilly road. The vast majority of the people pull on ropes to advance the coach. Quite often, they fall down into the mud and are trampled underfoot. A few riders on the top of the coach find themselves enjoying fresh air and pleasant vistas. Hunger drives the coach and mercilessly lashes those who pull the ropes. Those on top express sympathy for the "toilers of the rope" and offer the consolations of religion and charity to them. The riders on top worry they might lose their place on the coach, and some do so and are forced to start pulling. The coach is always in danger of "a general overturn in which all would lose their seats" (Bellamy 2007: 7).

Bellamy believes that the fundamental goodness of humanity will reveal itself once freed from the distortions of capitalist competition. In another allegory, the "Rose in the Bog," he compares humanity to a rose bush forced to grow in a dismal, pestilential swamp. Kept in the swamp by the conventional wisdom of "regular gardeners and moral philosophers," the plant withers. Once removed from this terrible place, the bush blooms, revealing its true nature, "covered with beautiful red roses, whose fragrance filled the world" (Bellamy 2007: 169).

In Bellamy's Boston, the state, and thus the people, control all property and means of production. Everyone who works or is retired enjoys a yearly guaranteed income (based on a sort of debit card). Bellamy assures us that this income is sufficient for anyone's needs, and since there is no need to save money people spend their whole income and maintain demand. Consumption becomes a positive value, since the problems of production have been solved. (Of course, the well-trained citizens of Boston practice admirable self-control.) Bellamy explains that every person deserves the same support from society and that to measure what people deserve by some standard of output is immoral.

Bellamy's utopian America organizes itself around the "Industrial Army." Work provides the key moral and organizing principle. All citizens, male and female, are subject to service from the ages of eighteen to forty-five. Women have their own separate army. (Bellamy shows little interest in explaining how this sort of gender apartheid functions.) He describes how his utopia has devised a system that satisfies the natural ambition of young men (not women). The most outstanding receive honors and recognition, including medals, ribbons and promotions in the Industrial Army. Patriotism and devotion to the greater good also motivate the men of the Industrial Army, just as they once inspired men in traditional military forces. Young men seek out dangerous "extra hazardous" work because they "are very greedy of honor, and do not let slip such opportunities" (Bellamy 2007: 41). Those who perform best reach the most important places of leadership. Bellamy makes it very clear that the superior man will seek to rise up through the ranks and that the "high places in the nation are open only to the highest-class men" (2007: 74). The men in Bellamy's utopia are in a continual race for honors and recognition. In this society, free riding, failing to pull your weight, is the greatest sin. Men who do so find themselves ostracized by their fellow citizens, especially by women.

Morris's Pastoral Utopia

Bellamy's *Looking Backward* inspired hundreds of utopian works. Some were sequels, some expanded points in the book, some attacked the book's militarized discipline and rather cold society. William Morris's *News from Nowhere* is considered the most important response to Bellamy. Born into wealth, Morris turned his back on the life of a leisured English aristocrat and devoted himself to the arts and radical politics. His life has been described as an effort "create, as best he saw how, a joyous, peaceful, and egalitarian *eu-topia* – not *nowhere* but a *good place*" (Robertson 2018: 130, original emphasis). Morris tried to "imagine the least tyrannous condition: the condition he believed allowed the greatest scope for individuals to determine the pattern of their own lives" (Kinna 2011: 291). If Bellamy's Boston harkens back to Sparta, Morris's England recalls the dream of Arcadia. Morris reacted with disgust against what he saw as the "narrow, complacent and authoritarian dimensions of *Looking Backward*." He saw Bellamy as a false prophet, a man of the middle class who was "perfectly satisfied with modern society," and who created a soulless "cockney paradise" of complacent consumerism (Robertson 2018: 78). For his part, Bellamy wrote a very positive review of *News from Nowhere* (See Bellamy 1891).

News from Nowhere represents "Morris's lifelong revolt against modernity" (Robertson, 2018: 114). A sleeper (a stand-in for the author) awakens in a future England that "is now a garden, where nothing is wasted and nothing is spoilt" (Morris 2004: 105). (Eventually the sleeper wakes up back in the filth and injustice of contemporary England.) The River Thames, once a byword for pollution, runs clear. Morris's utopians consciously reject technologies such as the steam engine. Even the use of the printing press has fallen out of favor. As one character says, "this is not an age of inventions. The last epoch did all that for us, and we are now content to use such of its inventions as we find handy, and leaving those alone which we don't want" (2004: 192). This selective use of technology becomes a recurring theme in green utopias.

As in *Looking Backward*, the reorganization of society, in particular the abolition of private property, has allowed true human values to come forth. Human nature, distorted by the imperatives of the market, by envy and by competition, reveals itself. People truly enjoy each other and the world around them. The polite form of address is "Neighbor," suggesting a world of friends and helpers. If duty provides the key principle in Bellamy's utopia, friendship seems to be the key principle for Morris. The people of this greener, more pleasant England live in anarchist libertarian communities. Citizens freely travel about the land, welcome to live anywhere they wish. There is no "state," no means of coercion beyond the power of public opinion and the need to earn one's own keep. There is no need for civil law since such laws existed to defend property and privilege. Freed from competition, the need to work merely to survive and the imposed slavery of "sham wants," the people once more take pride in the things they create. Eventually, all work becomes art. The people of this new England say: "at last and by slow degrees ... [we] got pleasure into our work; then we became conscious of that pleasure, and cultivated it" (Morris 2004: 160).

Morris dismisses all political struggles as "*pretended*" differences of opinion (2004: 117, original emphasis). These false differences collapse in the face of reasonable people recognizing mutual dependence. Once all questions are reduced to producing enough to meet the simple needs of the community, what else is left to fight about? What power is left to seize? Morris's utopians explicitly state that "we are very well off without politics – because we have none" (2004: 116). They have no disagreements that really matter: "Among us, our differences concern matters of business and passing events as to them, and could not divide men permanently." They have no disagreements that might motivate people to political action: "It is clearly not easy to knock up a political party on the question of whether haymaking in such and such a countryside shall begin this week or next" (2004: 118). In a piece of unsubtle satire, the former Houses of Parliament are used for the storage of dung.

Wells's Platonic Utopia

One of the most prolific writers of the late nineteenth and early twentieth centuries, H. G. Wells is considered one of the founders of the genre of science fiction. Wells foresaw a future of liberating scientific advance but feared both the destructive potential of human beings and their ability to devise false paradises (Kumar 1987: 174–86). In *A Modern Utopia*, Wells critiques the utopias of Morris and Bellamy. To make all work pleasing to human beings, he claims Morris has to change human nature in utterly implausible ways:

> I suppose we should follow Morris to his Nowhere, we should change the nature of man and the nature of things together;

we should make the whole race wise, tolerant, noble, perfect – wave our hands to a splendid anarchy, every man doing as it pleases him, and none pleased to do evil, in a world as good in its essential nature, as ripe and sunny, as the world before the Fall. (Wells 2005: 12)

Wells also notes the key problem with making work "fun." Quite simply, some work cannot be turned into pleasure. Wells rather nastily notes that "it is indeed the Olympian unworldliness of irresponsible rich man of the shareholding type … playing at life to imagine as much" (2005: 72). His critique of Bellamy is more subtle, but his continual reference to the freedom that his utopians have to work and live where and how they choose provides a clear counterpoint to the militarized discipline of *Looking Backward*.

Wells claims all utopias aim at "the complete emancipation of a community of men from tradition, from habits, from legal bonds, and that subtler servitude possessions entail" (2005: 13). To achieve this he, perhaps surprisingly, re-creates key features of Plato's *Republic*. The founders of the World State in *A Modern Utopia* succeed in "combining progress with political stability." As in Plato's Callipolis, the key to stability lies in a ruling class able to see the proper course for society. This elite, "the Samurai," shaped and established the World State (2005: 182, 176). They represent "the sovereignty not of the state, nor even of laws, but of scientific knowledge and collective enlightenment" (Kumar 1987: 218). As Wells notes, "such a world as this utopia is not made by the chance occasional co-operations of self-indulgent men, by autocratic rulers or by the bawling wisdom of the democratic leader" (2005: 118). The Samurai practice rigorous self-control and discipline. They co-opt and train those who are fitted to rule. In doing so, they maintain the stability of the World State, since all those who might have a desire to change society are brought into the ruling elite and indoctrinated into its ways. Like Plato's philosopher kings, the Samurai have discovered nearly infallible methods of identifying differing human characters and directing those characters in socially positive directions. The ambitions of those few who are capable of original thought (the "poietic" class) are "enabled and encouraged to give them a full development, in art, philosophy, invention or discovery" (2005: 184). The "voluntary nobility" of the Samurai, living under a rule designed to "produce maximum co-operation of all men of good intent," administer the state for the benefit of the "dull" and the "base." All power resides in them, and they are able, seemingly without fail, to assign good men to the tasks of administration (2005: 187, 188, 207).

But, to achieve this, the state continually monitors its citizens. Wells's World State is a prototype of the surveillance state. All citizens are indexed, and the system is so perfect "that two strangers cannot appear anywhere upon the planet without discovery" (2005: 118). Wells ignores the dangerous possibilities of such a system. He even seems quite proud of the idea. In effect, he substitutes state observation and monitoring for the public pressures and communally enforced norms of older utopias. He grants the World State control over reproduction. He devotes a chapter of the book to the place of women in utopia, and it is telling that most of the chapter delineates how the state directs marriage and child-bearing. The World State actively intervenes to arrange marriages for the eugenic improvement of the human race: "the State is to exercise the right of forbidding or sanctioning motherhood." Female infidelity is a crime against the State, since it might result in the production of inferior children, while male infidelity "is clearly of no importance whatsoever" (2005: 129, 133). Even the women who join the Samurai class are mostly defined as helpers to their husbands, who are doing the real work. While officially equal, women are subordinate objects, constrained for their own and the common good.

Wells would expand on the ideas of *A Modern Utopia* in *Men Like Gods* (1923). While he expressly says this utopia is located on another planet, its inhabitants are human, and it is possible this utopia might represent the future evolution of the World State. Wells claimed that, in this utopia, "all the people are Samurai" (quoted in Kumar 1987: 219). He says that "Earth, which was now no more than a wilderness, sometimes horrible and at best picturesque … would grow rich with loveliness" (1923: 315).

Gilman's Feminist Utopia

In *Herland*, Charlotte Perkins Gilman uses the utopian form to critique the unexamined ideas and practices of patriarchy. Gilman had a long career as lecturer and organizer for women's rights. Her famous short story "The Yellow Wallpaper" (1892) was a pioneering study of post-partum depression and a savage attack on the treatment of women's mental health by the male-dominated medical profession. She found Bellamy's ideas inspiring, especially Nationalism's promise to "liberate women from compulsory domesticity" (Robertson 2018: 173), and she believed that the recognition of women's rights would come about "through a joint effort of activist politics and radical fantasies" (Bammer 2015: 57).

Herland has many elements of the classic utopia, a voyage by outsiders (in this case, three men) to a new country, their education in the nature and functioning of the society, and their (possible) conversion to the new land's ways and beliefs. *Herland* fits into the utopian pattern of a communal society built around total unity and commitment. The all-female society of Herland is, in effect, a single family, descended from a single mother. All work solely for the common good over the long term, since the desires of the individual and the community are one. As one of the visitors says, "to them the country was a unit – it was Theirs. They themselves were a unit, a conscious group; they thought in terms of the community." They are able to make truly long-term plans, since "their time-sense was not limited to the hopes and ambitions of an individual life. Therefore, they habitually considered and carried out plans for improvement which might cover centuries." When one of the men explains that the "laws of nature require a struggle for existence," they find the concept repellent, since it condemns a large proportion of any society to misery (Gilman 1999: 80, 63).

The men who enter Herland find it a challenge to their basic understanding of the world. They believe that women are not capable of organizing an orderly society. The male interlopers continually "mansplain" the outside world to the astonished, shocked and often disgusted women of Herland. As their most cherished beliefs about the nature of world are revealed to be nothing more than prejudice, the men become less sure of themselves and less able to defend unexamined practices they have always accepted as "natural." They come to recognize that the women of Herland are not "feminine" because femininity is a male construct. Unlike the outside world, where male is equal to human and female is merely a secondary category, the women of this utopia are people first and foremost.

Gilman critiques contemporary patriarchal religion. The women of Herland ask, seemingly innocently, "Why is God a man?" Gilman's utopians have no idea of original sin. They find the idea of eternal punishment to be horrible and perverse and the idea of personal immorality strange and disturbing. Why worry about such things, they ask, when Herland already exists in a state of "Peace and Beauty, and Comfort and Love" (Gilman 1999: 116).

Herland presents a critique of the male-imposed position of subordination of women and of the many self-serving male assumptions about the nature of women. There are strong elements of satire. Each of the men presents an extreme caricature of contemporary male attitudes toward women. They continually attempt to assert their manly dominance, whether physically or intellectually, only to be easily overpowered by the women. Each of the intruders gets a lesson that demonstrates the absurdity of his desire for power and mastery.

Twentieth-Century Variants on the Theme

The production of literary utopias continues to this day, but the relative influence of such works has declined. But there are several post-World War II utopias that deserve our attention. B. F. Skinner's *Walden Two* (1948), Aldous Huxley's *Island* (1962) and Ernest Callenbach's *Ecotopia* (1975) all raise important questions about the place and purpose of utopian dreaming. In particular, Skinner's *Walden Two* provided the blueprint for a number of intentional communities, some of which survive to this day, most notably Twin Oaks in Virginia (Kuhlmann 2005).

Skinner presents a utopian commune based on modern methods of psychological conditioning. What most people call freedom, Skinner sees as a delusion blinding us to the horror of the true nature of human society and consoling us with the illusion of choice. A well-ordered society can do without such false freedom. Education in this community, as in Plato's Callipolis, will "set up certain behavioral processes which will lead the individual to design his own 'good' conduct when the time comes" (Skinner 2005: 96). In *Walden Two*, the nature of conditioning raises serious questions. While those adults who join the commune can be seen as exercising free and informed choice, what about children brought up in the community and conditioned to its norms from birth? Can they make informed choices about whether or not to continue as members when they become adults? Are they better off not facing such a choice? Skinner's utopia forces us to consider, once again, whether social stability is worth the costs imposed on individual human choice and action.

In *Island*, Huxley harkens back to More and places utopia on a fictional island (Pala) in the South Pacific. He blends Western ideas of political order (and public health) with Buddhist spiritualism to create a society where human beings are physically and psychologically healthy. The people are sexually open (at least in a heterosexual fashion) and experience enlightenment through the use of a particular drug. The Palans reject most modern technology and live in balance with nature. As in Plato's utopia, the result is a society in which change can only be seen as a movement away from perfection.

Huxley, like Skinner, sees mental conditioning as the key to utopian practice. Palan methods of education and training have, in the minds of its ruling elite, changed human biological programming in a way that transcends laws or political structures. The desire for power "has to be curbed on the legal and political levels ... but it's also obvious that there must be prevention on the individual level. On the level of emotion, on the level of glands and viscera, the muscles and the blood" (Huxley 1962: 180). Children who exhibit a desire to control and dominate (called "Peter Pans" and "Muscle Men") are treated with drugs and other methods.

As one character smugly puts it, "all the cute little Peter Pans are spotted without fail and appropriate treatment is started immediately" (1962: 176). Pala's leaders believe they have cured the problem of disruptive desire. But, as Tom Moylan summarizes the problem, "while a self-reflexive attention to process informs *personal* life in Pala, such a process of critique and regeneration never takes place at the societal level" (2014: 219, original emphasis).

The story ends on a depressing note. Pala cannot escape history. Its self-satisfaction means it ignores the dangers of the outside world. The utopia falls prey to the ambitions of a neighboring country. Pala is conquered and its leaders murdered. Huxley suggests that, in our present age, utopian experiments cannot succeed. The death of Pala is the death of utopia.

Produced during the first era of ecological consciousness and at the height of the sexual revolution, Callenbach's *Ecotopia* has many features of the classic utopia. A traveler once more comes to a mysterious land, is at first a skeptic, but is finally converted. The new nation of Ecotopia, comprising Northern California and the states of Oregon and Washington, has cut itself off from the rest of the United States. Ecotopia strives to create a "steady state" society, based on sustainable ecological principles, communal living, small-scale worker-controlled enterprises and resistance to hierarchical authority. (Callenbach later produced a prequel, *Ecotopia Emerging* (1981), which delineated the revolution that produced the Ecotopian state and society.)

As in other classic utopias, there is little private space in Ecotopia. Its citizens observe, comment upon, and censure each other's behavior, enforcing a soft, but real, conformity. "Mechanisms of moral persuasion" are universal in this society (Callenbach 1990: 21). The Ecotopians work for only a few hours a day. They seek to live in nature, seeing themselves as beings "meant to take their modest place in the seamless web of living organisms" (1990: 47). Sexual freedom is universal but, in the spirit of the 1970s sexual revolution, still focused on male liberation from repressive norms. Women, seen as nurturing and imbued with a sort of mystical feminine power, control the government and provide the ideological basis for the state. The government exists as a sort of wise technocracy directing investment toward earth-friendly high-tech sectors and managing trade with foreign countries. While the forms of electoral democracy are observed, long debates leading to consensus provide the preferred form of decision making. All enterprises are governed in this way. (Recently, utopian theorists have come to see deliberative democracy of this sort as a means for producing truly legitimate political decisions (Wenner 2017).)

Ecotopia critiques what is (or might be) and plans for something better. While the work is set in 1999, all the economic and political tendencies of the 1970s have continued. Dystopian conditions prevail in the remaining parts of the United States. The nation engages in endless wars, suffers from long-term economic stagnation, and is unable to prevent pollution from killing 30,000 people a year (citizens walk around in New York City wearing gas-masks). Draconian measures of population control seem to be in operation. Government secrecy is the norm, even allowing the United States to cover up a massive, failed military attack on Ecotopia. Meanwhile, the "Green Revolution" has failed, leading to general starvation in the Third World.

As a work of political thought, *Ecotopia* provides a window onto a particular era when the dreams of the early environmental movement and the ideology of individual, particularly sexual, liberation seemed to be the way of the future. But many of the features of Ecotopia, such as the worship of nature, the romanticizing of the American Indian, consequence-free sexual freedom and the idea of a benevolent elite directing technological change, have been rendered absurd or embarrassing in the last forty years. It might be impossible to recapture the naïve optimism that runs throughout the book. Perhaps that provides a reason for the decline of the literary utopia, why our society has become more cynical and more distrustful of both politics and our ability to direct economic or technological change to benefit humanity and the planet.

Utopia as a Process

Ursula K. Le Guin's "ambiguous utopia" *The Dispossessed* (1974) challenges and expands the idea of utopia. She addresses the difficulty of making the case for utopia in the face of the obvious dangers posed by ideologically driven social engineering. Can we still dream of creating societies of equality and unity? To address this question, Le Guin creates a "critical utopia," always "alert to the dangers and risks attached to static blueprints of perfect societies" (Thaler 2018: 685). The novel is a "challenge to the perfectionist conception of utopia as a timeless idyll dammed off forever against the wide river of history" (Davis 2005: 13). This utopia is far from perfect and is designed to be capable of self-reflection and change. It faces serious and perhaps unsolvable problems, but, at the same time, its ideals and the actions of its people serve as a source of hope and as an aspirational model. Le Guin wrestles with how a truly anarchist society could function and how freely directing individuals would act in such a community. She asks how a person can act in complete freedom and still work for the common good. How can the potentially divergent goals of maximum personal liberty and a just and equitable society be realized? How does power corrupt even in a society where the power to corrupt is not supposed to exist?

Le Guin contrasts two societies, the anarchist utopia of the planet Anarres and the rich, yet unequal society of Io on the planet Urras. Io can be seen as a stand-in for the United States. In a twist on most utopian works, a traveler moves from utopia to dystopia. An Anarrean scientist visits Urras. At first he sees Io as utopian, but over time he comes to see the dystopian nature of a capitalist society built on exploitation, alienation and state violence.

Like Utopia, Anarres is a place where no one starves, everyone is housed and clothed, almost everyone has meaningful work, and merit, defined as what one contributes to society through their labor, not wealth, determines public esteem. The people of Anarres have attained one of the key goals of all utopias, detaching a person's standing in society from money or some other "accidental" feature.

While obsessively anarchist, society on Anarres employs many methods to enforce unity and move individuals toward proper social action. Education prevents self-interest ("egoism"). Propaganda reminds the people of the continual threat posed by Urras. The community applies intense pressure on individuals to accept work that serves collective needs. The Anarreans are expected to demonstrate total commitment to the common good. Le Guin suggests that Anarres does not fully live up to its ideals and has become increasingly conformist. Its inhabitants accept its central myth and ignore evidence that shows individual self-direction under attack by conformity. They delude themselves that, since there is no "state" to enforce laws, there can be no coercion in their society. The anarchists of Anarres become ruled more and more ruled by the unspoken yet overwhelming power of the majority. They "have become unused to the very idea of anyone's adopting a course harmful to others and persisting in it against advice and protest." They have forgotten that "any rule is tyranny" (Le Guin 2011: 355, 359). Submission to the power of the majority is a surrender of freedom and responsibility. But many of them see it as a sort of liberation. Better to mouth conventional and acceptable ideas than to stand out and be crushed by the weight of public opinion. Over time the assertion of individual goals has come to be seen as antisocial and irresponsible. Society demands that the ambitious "abandon initiative in return for receiving approval" (2011: 355, 378). Power adheres to institutions, and "the center ceases to serve and change as needed and instead holds to the status quo for the sake of the permanent elite in the bureaucracy" (Moylan 2014: 96). Social pressures enforce conformity and a fetishizing of the "state" ideology. Some individuals seek power within the ostensibly anarchic system. Unity, once defined as freely choosing to work together, has come mean accepting the power of opinion. The idea of permanent revolution, of continuous change and questioning, falters.

Le Guin asks us to recognize the trade-offs that must be made in any utopia. Not all desires can be attained. Individual freedom must sometimes, even for anarchists, be sacrificed to the common good. Utopia is not perfection. Utopia is a process. It is a movement toward the goals of all utopian thought, equality and unity. The problem of Anarres lies in how to restart that process. At the end of the book the traveler returns to Anarres aware of the failings of both societies and more committed to restoring the foundational principles of his community.

Toward Dystopia

We are a long way from the intellectual playfulness of More's *Utopia*. In the nineteenth and twentieth centuries, demanding the impossible came to be seen as fraught with dangers and disappointments. The bold visions of Bellamy, Morris, Wells and Gilman receded as real events revealed the dangerous possibilities of utopian dreaming. Skinner and Huxley attempt to resituate the utopia, whether in a small community or once more in a distant land, but neither seems confident that utopian experiments can survive in the face of raw power, whether of the majority or of the predatory nation-state. Callenbach's vision of green utopia seems naïve in the face of current realities. More hopefully, Le Guin poses a new question. What if utopia is an open-ended process, never completed, always in question? She provides a template for any plausible utopian narrative. But the trends in utopian thought have shifted. Bellamy's and Wells's work culminated a kind of utopian thought, one that placed great faith in the ability of a detached scientific or technocratic elite to direct society for the common good. Reactions against this model of utopia had already been seen in Morris's *News from Nowhere* and would become more commonplace as utopian thought faced the dangerous possibilities (and realities) of unrestrained state power. This reaction finally leads to dystopian or anti-utopian works, the most prevalent form of twentieth-century utopian thought. Dystopia or anti-utopia warns against efforts at changing human nature or reshaping human society.

In the twentieth century, while literary utopias turned toward dystopia, utopian thought became the subject of academic debate. Scholars began to ask whether utopian thought constituted a new form of political ideology or was itself a challenge to existing political ideologies. They began to ask if the term "utopian" could be applied to existing ideologies.

6
Utopia and/as Ideology

Can we consider utopian political thought an ideology? Does utopian political thought constitute a truly organized system of belief? What practical effects result from treating utopia as an ideology? But before addressing those questions it is important to ask: just what is ideology? "An ideology is a system of values and beliefs regarding the various institutions and processes of a society that is accepted as a fact or truth by a group of people. An ideology provides the believer with a picture of the world both as it is and as it should be, and, in doing so, it organizes the tremendous complexity of the world into something fairly simple and understandable" (Sargent 2009: 2). Ideology is a means to shape reality. It also distorts reality by preventing believers from seeing the contradictions and problems caused by their own beliefs. Quite often ideology reduces human beings to abstractions and discounts their individual value in favor of some greater goal.

In *Ideology and Utopia* (1936), Karl Mannheim described the relationship between utopia and ideology as part of the conflict between rulers and the ruled. Those who suffer under oppressive social orders use utopian thought to challenge their conditions of existence. Utopian thought helps them codify their demands for change and ultimately paves the way for revolutionary action. Ruling classes use ideology to justify their power, often claiming that the current organization of society is right, just and natural and that any changes to it are both dangerous and quite likely impossible. Mannheim says they "will label as utopian all conceptions of existence which *from their point of view* can in principle never be realized" (1991: 176–7, original emphasis). But he stresses that we must recognize that neither utopia nor ideology provides "accurate descriptions of the world" and that they must always be tested against reality, even if reality itself is unstable (Sargent 2008). However, using utopia as a means to critique a dominant ideology faces what is called the "Mannheim Paradox." It points out a basic problem: "how does one understand an ideology from inside one" (Sargent 2013: 445). In *Lectures on Ideology and Utopia* (1986), Paul Ricoeur seeks to escape this paradox by claiming that utopia creates a place or standpoint that allows us to understand and critique the ideologies that surround us and influence our lives. "From this 'no place' an exterior glance is cast on reality, which suddenly looks strange, nothing more being taken for granted. The field of the possible is now open beyond that of the actual" (1986: 16). Seen this way, utopian thought is profoundly anti-ideological, since it always questions and attacks the dominant beliefs of the times.

But we can also consider utopian thought as ideological, since it provides organizing values and beliefs. "Utopia is always an ideology ... it is the driving ideology of history, the ideology that moves things beyond the current state of things" (Fischbach 2016: 124). And so "there is a utopia at the heart of every ideology, a positive picture – some vague, some quite detailed – of what the world would look like if the hopes of the ideology were realized" (Sargent 2010: 124). Feminist utopian thought employs ideology to challenge ideology. A new ideology of human equality and female empowerment challenges and critiques the unconsciously accepted idea of male supremacy.

Utopia is anti-ideological and ideological. Utopia can be ideology, but it is also a thing that exists alongside ideology and challenges existing world views. Utopia helps to overthrow existing ideologies but always seems on the verge of becoming one itself. Seemingly realized utopias, whether they are literary experiments or real-life communities, exhibit the features of static and unchanging ideological solutions.

As Lyman Tower Sargent says, "today ideology and utopia are best seen as intimately connected in that there is a utopia at the heart of every ideology because all ideologies have some notion of the better world that will come about if the ideology is fully implemented. ... But is it important to recognize that however closely related they may be, they are not the same" (2013: 447).

Two potentially utopian ideologies of modern times are Marxian socialism and libertarianism. They demanded (and still demand) the impossible (or at least what seems impossible). Both provide a means to critique and possibly replace the existing order of society. Both are deeply suspicious of democracy, albeit for different reasons. Marxian socialism and libertarianism are anti-political, favoring other means of dispute resolution. They claim to reflect true human nature. Karl Marx claims that what we perceive as human nature really reflects that economic organization of society. Libertarians such as Milton Friedman claim that free markets are a reflection of human nature, that capitalism is itself a natural product. Libertarians replace traditional utopian demands for the abolition of private property and the establishment of equality with demands for freedom of choice. They see the free market as a means of overcoming the power of the state. Libertarians see the state, especially in the expanded modern form, as the main impediment to utopia. Robert Nozick (1974) attempted to reconcile libertarian ideas with utopian concepts by delineating the "minimal state," a set of small communities of total commitment and total freedom. In contrast, socialists see the state (even if, for Marx, it might "wither away" at some future time) as a means to attain utopian goals.

The relationship between utopian thought and political ideology remains contentious. Totalitarian ideas are often identified as utopian. In response, there have been efforts to create links between utopia and Marxism that open space for dreams and action outside of the state, as seen in the work of Ernst Bloch. Others have simply rejected utopia as a meaningful ideological category in light of the horrors of the twentieth century (Jacoby 2005: 73–82).

Marx/Marxism as Utopian

Marx and Marxists employed the scientific claims of Marxism, especially its supposed predictive power, to separate themselves from the so-called utopian socialists. In the *Communist Manifesto* (1848) Marx and his collaborator Friedrich Engels objected to the utopian socialists' plans to "establish islands of socialism in a sea of capitalism" (Geoghegan 1987: 15). They believed that such reformist plans failed to understand the struggle between classes and ultimately relied on the goodwill of capitalists such as Robert Owen to fund a sort of paternalistic socialism. They also believed that the utopian socialists failed to accept the need for the total transformation of society and claimed they limited their demands to small changes designed to make capitalism less exploitative. Utopian socialists were reformers who wanted "the bourgeoisie [the ruling class of capitalism] without the proletariat [the working class]." Their experimental communities were "pocket editions of the new Jerusalem" that could never succeed in the face of the pressures imposed by capitalism (Marx 1996b: 24, 26). Marx and Engels saw the ideas and projects of the utopian socialists as essentially impractical, romantic and reactionary, ignoring the historical forces shaping the developing consciousness of the working class and producing "a specially contrived organization of society" detached from actual practice. While Marx and Engels do note that the utopian socialists brought forward useful proposals for the "transformation" of the family, of property rights, of wage-labor and for state control of production, they claim that all such proposals fail because they reject the reality of the class struggle and thus the need for fundamental revolutionary change (1996b: 27–8).

The debate between Karl Marx and the people he pejoratively labeled utopian socialists says more about Marx and the petty power and purity struggles of activist politics than it does about utopian thought or socialism. Marx wanted to establish himself as the only "true" or "correct" source of socialist ideas. As is usual with such battles, minor differences in dogma or plans of action are inflated, and fights within a small group come to take on apocalyptic meaning. Vincent

Geoghegan summarized the dispute, saying that Marx and Engels's "desire to stress the political distinctiveness of their own stance led them to be less than fair to their 'utopian' predecessors" (1987: 29). Krishan Kumar notes "the many features Marxism took over from the utopians: from Saint-Simon, the slogan 'from the government of men to the administration of things' and the idea of the 'withering away' of the state from Fourier, the idea that 'in any given society the degree of the emancipation of women is the natural measure of general emancipation' from Owen" (1987: 52).

An examination of Marx's analysis of capitalism and his list of demands in the *Communist Manifesto* provides a concrete starting point to query the utopian nature of Marxism. But there are other elements of Marxist thought to consider. We must examine Marx's understanding of history, his idea of human nature and, finally, his conception of justice. All three are critical parts of any utopian critique and project.

Marx saw history as moving toward the establishment of communism. Modern capitalism creates the conditions for its own destruction, even as it moves from success to success. In some ways Marx seems to have more faith in capitalism than the capitalists of his own time. In his view, capitalism has unleashed more productive forces than any other form of social and economic organization. Its monumental success allows humanity, for the first time, to escape the limits of nature. At the same time, capitalism's very success proves its undoing. Marx says that "modern bourgeois society, which has conjured up such powerful means of production and trade, resembles the sorcerer who could no longer control the unearthly powers he had summoned forth" (1996b: 6). Capitalism continually undermines and overthrows all existing structures of social organization. Nothing is ever secure, even for capitalists. Capitalism's continual economic crises drive members of the ruling bourgeoisie into the ranks of the working class. Successful enterprises come to control more and more of the market and create monopolies. Workers become more and more miserable in the face of economic and state power that serves the interests only of the bourgeoisie.

Marx's describes contemporary capitalist society as a (tenuous) utopia for the bourgeoisie and as a dystopia for the ever more oppressed proletariat. He also describes how the ever-growing misery of the workers will drive them to a recognition of their power as a class. They will come to see the claims about human nature and the so-called natural order of society made by church and state as mere justifications for oppression. When this moment occurs, they will come to see the necessity of revolution and the inarguable logic of the communist program spelled out in the *Manifesto*.

In the *Manifesto*, Marx and Engels present a series of specific demands that could be considered utopian in the context of 1848. They demanded a progressive tax system, the abolition of inheritance, national control over banking, state control of transportation, universal national service in the form of industrial armies, universal, free public education and the end of child labor (Marx 1996b: 19–20). Perhaps most importantly, they demanded the abolition of private property. They note that property, defined as the ownership of the means of production such as land, factories and stocks and the control of banks, has already been effectively abolished for almost the entire population of capitalist countries (1996b: 15). Abolishing private property ends the connection between power and money. Money is a corrupting influence, since it has the power to bend and shape our very perception of reality. Capitalism has reduced all human values to "naked self-interest, [to] unfeeling 'hard cash'" (1996b: 3). Money provides the only means to assign value to religion, to the family and to every sort of human relation.

In other works, Marx defended his theories against the claim that the triumph of communism would lead to universal laziness and free riding. He says that communism will change the very nature of work. Labor under capitalism is always "coerced, *forced labour.*" The worker experiences his work as "external" as "not part of his very being." Since his work is merely repetitive, unthinking physical action, "he does not affirm himself but denies himself, feels miserable instead of satisfied, does not freely exercise and develop physical and intellectual energy but mortifies his body and ruins his mind" (Marx 1994: 73, original emphasis). A successful proletarian revolution will end these conditions. Since capitalism requires the exploitation of labor for profit, ending capitalism ends exploitation. All labor will then serve the common good and the good of the individual worker. Once labor ceases to be alienating, once exploitation has ended, human beings would once more express their full nature through their work. Once conditions of exploitation end, true human freedom becomes possible. Free of class conflicts, society becomes "an association in which the free development of each is the condition for the free development of all" (Marx 1996b: 20). Our true nature as creative beings, denied us by capitalism, will be realized.

Is Marxian socialism/communism utopian? In line with much of the utopian tradition, it aims for a new form of economic and social organization free from inequality. Humanity attains true justice, in the sense that all people are treated as subjects with value, not merely as instruments of production and profit. As Kumar says, "a society of material abundance, a society which has banished alienation and exploitation, a society in which all men and women relate to each other as artists to their creations: such a conception is in most essential aspects utopian (and none the worse for it)" (1991: 60–1). Claeys suggests a number of reasons we should consider Marx a utopian. First, he says that Marx follows the tradition established by More's *Utopia*, since both give "priority to sociability over property ownership and to the public over the private." Second, Marx opposes specialization in labor and its division into physical and mental labor. Third, he assumes, again in line with classic utopian thought, that "social behavior would improve dramatically once private property ended." Fourth, Marx saw communal property as the original and perhaps most natural form of human social organization. Fifth, he expected his ideas to overcome the problem of "scale" that faces utopian thought. Marx believed "that advances in socialization, notably mitigating coercion and oppression, which were doubtless achievable in small-scale communities, could be emulated at the level of the nation state" (Claeys 2018: 153–6). (The scalability of utopia remains an open question to this day.) Finally, in line with earlier utopians, Marx saw his system as the culmination of human development. He "believed that the direction of historical development was a purposeful one determined by the interplay of material forces, and would come to an end only with the achievement of a communist utopia that would finally resolve all prior contradictions" (Fukuyama 1989: 4).

But any discussion of the whether or not Marx can be considered a utopian must face his well-known rejection of the term and his constant refusal to provide blueprints for a future socialist society. He claimed that his theory, unlike those of the utopian socialists, was free from romantic notions about the creation of a harmonious world. He saw his theories as part of a dynamic social and political process, not simply a set of predictions or guidelines. In the afterword to the second edition of *Capital* (1873), he emphatically rejected demands for "receipts [recipes] for the cookshops of the future" (1996a: 17). Since Marx believed a true socialist state was far in the future, describing it in minute detail would be impossible and presumptuous. Indeed, to do so would be counterproductive, since it would create unnecessary divisions in the diverse transnational working-class revolutionary movement he was trying to build (1996b: 29–30). Much of Marx's thought was directed to goals that have been called utopian, or appeared utopian in the context of the times. But Marx believed that attaining those goals required a hard-headed realism, stripped of romantic notions, recognizing that conflict between the classes would drive and shape history, not artful plans or pious philanthropy.

Ernst Bloch: Hope and Dreams

Most orthodox Marxists strongly rejected the label "utopian." They, like Marx, saw utopian dreaming as unsystematic, "unscientific" and fundamentally unserious. But there have been notable efforts to reconceptualize utopian thought and reconcile it with Marxism. Perhaps the most interesting effort in this direction came from the German philosopher Ernst Bloch, who attempted to "rehabilitate utopia *within Marxism* as a neglected Marxist category" (Levitas 1990: 14, original emphasis). For Bloch, utopia became a "philosophy of hope and an act of will" (Claeys 2018: 151). Its "anticipatory consciousness" allows us to imagine "possibilities that have not yet been – but could eventually be – realized" (Bammer 2015: 3). Bloch saw utopia appearing in almost all forms of human experience. In his massive work *The Principle of Hope* (1954–9), he "likened utopia to daydreams" that show us a "plurality of visions to reflect the desired plurality of everyday experience in both the real and ideal worlds" (Segal 2012: 251). He makes utopia a part of our shared human experience. It is necessary, natural and everywhere. In this way, we are all utopians. Geoghegan summarizes why Bloch's work matters: "his achievement was to see that utopianism is not confined to intellectuals and their various blueprints of a better life. He saw that, in countless ways, individuals are expressing unfulfilled dreams and aspirations – that in song and dance, plants and plaster, church and theatre, utopia waits" (1987: 97).

Bloch's most useful contribution to utopian theory lies in his distinction between the abstract and concrete utopia. Abstract utopia, understood as thought experiments, has its place, but is insufficient. As Ruth Levitas explains, "abstract utopia is fantastic and compensatory. It is wishful thinking, but the wish is not accompanied by a will to change anything" (1990: 14–15). Concrete utopias are "outlines of a better world." They are "dreaming, stripped of illusion" (Geoghegan 1987: 93, 94). They require us to face the current reality that exists, not merely wish it away. They perform the "essential utopian function, that of simultaneously anticipating and effecting the future" (Levitas 1990: 15). Even the most hardheaded "realist" needs to engage in utopian dreaming, because without the dream there can be no action. But without concrete planning and design, action fails to produce a positive outcome.

Libertarianism as Utopian Ideology

Like Marxism, libertarianism makes claims of scientific rationality for its preferred system. Libertarianism also claims to have discovered the best form of human interaction. Free markets are natural and support liberty, since they are an outgrowth of uncoerced individual action. Libertarian utopia is based on the idea that all forms of coercion are illegitimate. No individual can be forced, even for her own good, to live or act in ways that are not freely chosen. But almost any government we can imagine will act in a coercive fashion. For libertarians, socialism is based on state coercion and democracy is founded on the principle that a political majority has a moral right to coerce a political minority. They equate political democracy with tyranny of the majority. As Milton Friedman said: "the believer in freedom has never counted noses" (1982: 9). So, a libertarian utopia will be designed to limit the ability of majorities to enforce their will. The state will be as minimal as possible, leaving most decisions to the market, where, in theory, coercion is impossible since diverse choices and desires can be accommodated, unlike the mostly binary choices presented by democracy.

While libertarian ideas can be traced back to various forms of anarchist capitalism, Friedman's *Capitalism and Freedom* (1962) lays the foundation of libertarianism as a utopian political program. The book might properly be called the "capitalist manifesto." Friedman notes a paradox at the heart of all governments. While government is necessary to preserve freedom and rights, especially property rights, government is also the greatest danger to human liberty. In order to preserve liberty, the power of the state must be limited. Its legitimate functions include national defense, maintaining law and order, enforcing private contracts, preventing monopolies and protecting property rights (Friedman 1982: chap. 2). Any further actions by the state are suspect, especially if they are justified by "paternalism," which Friedman defines as the belief that individuals don't know their best interests. Since free individual choice is the highest good, any limitation of that freedom cannot be justified.

In what might be a conscious imitation of Marx, Friedman presents a libertarian program, a set of demands for the limitation of the state and the rollback of government intervention. Like Marx's program in the *Manifesto*, many of Friedman's demands would have seemed impossible in 1962, but many of his points, like those of Marx, have been attained. For example, Friedman called for the end of conscription, of government regulation of transportation and communication, of rent control and price and wage controls, and of government control of output in the agricultural and energy sectors (1982: 35–6). The rise of conservative governance in the 1980s in the United States and Great Britain produced many of these changes.

Friedman and libertarianism replace the traditional utopian ideals of equality and unity with choice and individual liberty. But the goal is the same: a society in which outcomes are just, in which people receive what they deserve. And, like other utopian theories, libertarianism seeks to devalue politics as the guiding force in society.

Designing Libertarian Utopia

In his *Anarchy, State and Utopia* (1974), Robert Nozick proposes a libertarian framework for the minimal state, one in which individual liberty will be compromised the least. He outlines the creation of large numbers of small communities of shared interest. Like other utopian communities, they will be founded by "visionaries and crackpots, maniacs and saints, monks and libertines, capitalists and communists and participatory democrats." Nozick applies market principles to the building of communities. People will seek out social/political/economic groupings that best fit their needs. Reflecting the free market, "some communities will be abandoned, others will struggle along, others will split, others will flourish, gain membership, and be duplicated elsewhere" (1974: 316). Individuals will move from one community to another in search of maximal good. (Nozick does not address the problem of children who are brought up in a community and know no other alternative.) Each mini-utopia would be the "best possible world for each person living in that world" (Bader 2011: 258).

Nozick theorizes the creation of "stable associations" in which individual liberty might be compromised, so long as this surrender is voluntary and exit is free. There should be "a wide and diverse range of communities which people can enter if they are admitted, leave if they wish to, shape according to their wishes; a society in which utopian experimentation can be tried, different styles of life can be lived, and alternative visions of the good can be individually and jointly pursued." He notes that, while "the framework is libertarian and laissez-faire, *individual communities within it need not be*" (1974: 320, original emphasis). The key principle is that no person or group could coercively impose a particular utopian vision on any other person or group.

Nozick's theory reflects a bias against protest and political activity that lies at the heart of classical utopia. Disagreement will be resolved by individuals leaving the community and finding a more congenial one. Nozick avoids the dangers of totalizing utopian ideology by narrowing the reach of any single belief system. In Nozick's stable associations, the individual must contract away her autonomy, at least conditionally, to some communal ideal, however limited in scope. But, in a politics conditioned by concern for individual rights, perhaps these are the only utopias we can honestly design. John Gray claims that only small-scale utopian communities can avoid oppressing the individual: "the pursuit of Utopia need not end in totalitarianism. So long as it is confined to voluntary communities it tends to be self-limiting" (2007: 39).

Utopia as Liberation

Utopian dreaming allows oppressed and subordinated groups and peoples to imagine and prepare mental and material spaces of resistance. Two important places in which this mode of thought shows its necessity and vitality are feminism and post- or anti-colonialism.

All feminist thought has utopian aspects. What is more utopian than the demand that women be treated as freely directing individuals? After all, there is no more universal ideology of oppression than male superiority and female subordination. Feminist utopian thought allows its authors to act as "Authoresses of a whole world" (Cavendish 2003: 109). Angelika Bammer suggests that Christine de Pizan's *Book of the City of the Ladies* (1404) could be considered the first modern utopian work, since it challenges the assumptions of patriarchy and imagines a better world for women (2015: 16, 37–8). Ruth Levitas says that "feminism is fundamentally informed by the view that the world should be otherwise" (2013: 95). Since "gender equality has never fully existed, so it must be imagined if it is to become the subject of conscious thought and discussion" (Johns 2010: 175). Feminist thought understands patriarchy as unnatural, despite its being a nearly universal condition. In reaction to the classic utopian form laid out by More that has supported (mostly unreflectively) the subordination of women, feminist utopian thought focuses on process and critique. Utopian feminist thought is "not marked by closure ... it builds, advances and applies a new approach to utopianism" (Sargisson 1996: 4). Bammer argues that utopianism always informs feminism and that, "at the very time the dream of utopia was being pronounced dead [the 1970s], it was vibrantly alive in the emergent American and western European women's movements" (2015: 2). Lucy Sargisson notes that contemporary feminist utopian fiction represents the "continuing *desire for change*; the continuing desire to desist from old patterns of thought and behavior" (2012: 78, original emphasis).

Manifestos of women's rights activists can be seen as utopian. Mary Wollstonecraft's *A Vindication of the Rights of Woman* (1792) can be understood as an imaginative reconstruction of society demanding women be understood "in the grand light of human creatures, who, in common with men, are placed on this earth to unfold their faculties" (1995: 75). The *Declaration of Sentiments* (1848) of the famous Seneca Falls Convention uses ideology (the claim of human equality in the Declaration of Independence) against ideology (the belief in the natural subordination of women). It lays out the dystopian condition of women in the face of the absolute power of men and demands that the natural equality of the sexes be recognized in law and in practice.

Despite appearing in many styles, explicitly utopian feminist literature always focuses on the same goal, treating women as freely acting subjects. Of course, the paths laid out to that goal can vary radically, ranging from matriarchal societies to pocket utopias in larger dystopias. The Indian author Rokeya Hossain's "Sultana's Dream" (1905) inverts the traditional societal order, placing women in a dominant position. The work shows the early adaptation of utopian thought by women in colonized places. Marge

Piercy's *Woman on the Edge of Time* (1976) exemplifies how feminist utopianism employs both dystopian visions of female oppression with utopian (but not naïve) dreams of full equality and understanding between genders. Sally Miller Gearhart's *Wanderground* (1978) takes different position, advocating for a utopia of female separatism. In a reflection of the rising prominence of dystopian literature in recent times, works such as Louise Erdrich's *Future Home of the Living God* (2017) imagine worlds of environmental degradation linked to the oppression of women. Advancing reproductive technologies increase the (often racially coded) economic divide between rich and poor women as governments increasingly monitor and control women's reproductive choices (Roberts 2009). The prospect of a "reproductive dystopia" is seen in works such as Leni Zumas's *Red Clocks* (2018) and Meg Elison's *Book of the Unnamed Midwife* (2017).

Utopian thought finds its origins, in part, in European colonialism. Settler colonies were often founded on the idea of creating new and just societies, refuges from a dangerously imperfect world. In response, victims of colonialism also employed utopian concepts and structures as forms and means of resistance. Bill Ashcroft claims that post- or anti-colonial utopianism is a universal phenomenon: "postcolonial utopianism arises from an unrecognized but powerful reality: that successful resistance is transformative, and transformation rests on the belief in an achievable future" (2017: 4). Such utopianism seeks to create a useful history against the colonizer's view that history starts with their arrival. Post-colonial utopia tries to reclaim the past in service of the future. Ironically, this future often expresses itself in the formation of a nation-state (itself a utopian construction) opposed to the colonizer's nation-state. This has often led to disappointment, as weak and arbitrarily delineated states fail to meet the utopian expectations of their founders. Ashcroft suggests that, in response to the shortcomings of the nation-state model, post-colonial authors seek to create a homeland, a place of true belonging, of deeper connection, of continual questioning, that goes beyond merely static political bonds (2017: 35–9).

The ideas of Gandhi for the construction of an independent India can be considered a prototype for anti-colonial utopianism. His *Hind Swaraj* (1909) presented a utopian picture of an independent India liberated from the pernicious influences of nationalism and Enlightenment modernity (Gandhi 1996). A new India would be built around "small communities in which each of the main groups, or *varna*, of Indian society would fulfil its defined role in cooperation with all of the other groups" (Sargent 2010: 73). These communities would practice self-reliance and thereby avoid entanglements with outside, colonizing forms of power. The tradition Hindu principles of "virtue, righteousness and duty to oneself and society" would guide society toward "equal rights and socio-religious freedom in a true democracy" (Dutton 2010: 240).

Modern anti-colonial utopianism is often seen in secession movements or movements to restore lost national independence. Independence movements in Catalonia, Quebec, Scotland and Tibet, to name just a few, paint pictures of a utopian past free from foreign oppression and a utopian future of economic, political and cultural liberation.

Whither Utopian Thought?

Intellectuals often make the mistake of believing that ideas drive history. Ideas matter. They can inspire; they can show people ways of thinking that challenge dominant paradigms; they provide the basis for claims against power and demands for change. But ideas do not make people do anything. Ideas do not force human beings to murder, to rape and to torture. Blaming any set of ideas for the horrors we have inflicted on each other represents a failure to confront human beings and the darkness that lies within all of us. Ideas can be used to justify actions, but we can be sure that Stalin, Mao, Hitler, Pol Pot and their kind would have found some other set of ideas to justify their horrific crimes. Saying these men and their ideas were "utopian" serves to foreclose the possibility of utopian dreaming and action.

Utopian thought is too often presented as a binary choice between "totalitarian perversion and otherworldly dreaming" (Ingram 2016: xix). Karl Popper claimed that all utopian speculation is built around an ideal of "totalitarian justice," enforced on all without regard to human nature or physical and political reality. For Popper, "utopian engineering" leaves us no choice but to try to build a society around "belief in one absolute and unchanging ideal." The inevitable outcome in such cases is an "attempt to create a strong centralized rule of a few, and which is likely to lead to dictatorship" (2013: 148–51). Jacob Talmon (1985) saw "totalitarian coercion" as a necessity in utopian thought, since any state organized on utopian principles requires complete agreement that can only be established by dictatorship. For many, the word "utopian" is inextricably linked with gulags and massive levels of state violence in pursuit of an ideological goal. As Geoghegan explains, the linkage of Marxism with Stalinism allowed the political right to "sell the equation: totalitarianism = Stalinism = Marxism = utopianism" (1987: 73). He also says that "liberals are quite right in seeing Auschwitz as the poisonous fruit of utopianism." But he goes on to claim that "they spoil their argument by arguing that Auschwitz is the inevitable consequence of utopianism" (1987: 4).

Otherworldly dreaming produces utopian theory that is disengaged from political action. This form of inquiry, often called critical theory, recognizes the deadly effects of the total reconstitution of societies around any dominant ideology and devotes "more attention to ensuring its nondogmatic, epistemically provisional status than its social content, let alone its politics" (Ingram 2016: xix). As such, critical theory cannot provide a path to concrete utopia. As Ruth Levitas notes, "utopia survives, but at a cost, and that cost is the retreat of the utopian function from transformation to critique" (2000: 25).

In reaction to these trends, utopian thought has moved in an anti-utopian or dystopian direction. Perhaps the most lively form of utopian dreaming has become identified with dystopia. The next two chapters consider the rise of dystopia as a form of utopian theory and what future utopian thought may have in face of our current crises.

7
From Utopia to Dystopia

Like utopian thought, dystopian thought reflects the concerns of its times. Dystopia critiques current conditions and warns against tendencies that might lead to potentially disastrous outcomes. Fyodor Dostoevsky's "The Grand Inquisitor" from *The Brothers Karamazov* (1880), E. M. Forster's "The Machine Stops" (1909) and Ursula K. LeGuin's "The Ones Who Walk Away from Omelas" (1973) provide templates for examining key concepts in dystopian works, such as the redefinition of freedom and the problems of technology, human isolation and the revelation of evil at the heart of a seemingly utopian society. The key twentieth-century dystopian works, such as *We* (1924), by the former Bolshevik revolutionary turned anti-Soviet exile Yevgeny Zamyatin, Aldous Huxley's *Brave New World* (1932), George Orwell's *Nineteen Eighty-Four* (1949) and Margaret Atwood's *The Handmaid's Tale* (1985), consider how the tendencies of their times could lead to tyrannical regimes. In contemporary times, the looming problems of the post-human and climate change drive dystopian thought.

The twentieth-century decline in production of the traditional utopias was mirrored by the rise of dystopian or anti-utopian works. Anti-utopian thought has existed for as long as utopian thought, as seen in the satirical responses to Plato's *Republic* by the playwright Aristophanes and that of Jonathan Swift in *Gulliver's Travels* to Francis

Bacon's rational scientific utopia *New Atlantis* (Kumar 1987: 99–100). But a specific form of dystopian thought and literature arose in the twentieth century. Dystopia "is largely the product of the terrors of the twentieth century. A hundred years of exploitation, repression, state violence, war, genocide, disease, famine, ecocide, depression, debt, and the steady depletion of humanity through the buying and selling of everyday life provided more than enough fertile ground for this fictive underside of the utopian imagination" (Moylan 2000: ix). Dystopia demands we examine our moral categories and judgments. Dystopian authors call our attention to the use and abuse of language for repressive proposes. They ask us to reconsider our assumptions about human nature and the limits of politics. Utopian thought needs dystopia. Dystopian thought warns against the dangers of utopian ideologies. Dystopia can be an "attempt to show, by as graphic and detailed a portrayal as possible, the horror of a society in which utopian aspirations have been fulfilled" (Kumar 1987: 109).

Dystopias are projections of existing negative trends. Lyman Tower Sargent defined dystopia as "a non-existent society described in considerable detail and normally located in time and space that the author intended a contemporaneous reader to view as considerably worse that the society in which that reader lived" (1994: 9). Russell Jacoby said "dystopias seek to frighten by accentuating contemporary trends that threaten freedom" (2005: 13). Margaret Atwood describes dystopias as projections of current events carried to their logical extremes. In this way, "every dystopia is a history of the future" (Lepore 2017).

Hope provides the essential focus of utopian thought. Fear provides the essential focus in dystopia. As Gregory Claeys says, "the central theme of the modern dystopia is despotism," producing "the estrangement and isolation of individuals, and their fear of each other" (2017: 290). The true horror of dystopia lies in the loss of trust among human beings. In a dystopian state people cannot join together to challenge the conditions of their existence. Throughout the classic dystopian works the hero or heroine is isolated, unsure of the meaning and purpose of existence, left to their own devices in the face of overwhelming force directed against them. Individuals in dystopias are under constant surveillance by the state and its agents. Human freedom is redefined to mean subjection. If utopia is based on shared human experience, solidarity and fraternity, dystopia is based on atomization, isolation and disconnection. History is erased, altered and invented. Detached from their fellow human beings, dystopian subjects are also cut off from the stream of time, living in an endless now that provides no resources to imagine how things could be different. Dystopian thought presents an inverted picture of community. Instead of the total commitment demanded in utopia, alienation and a general lack of intimate connection (friendship, love) are the characteristics of dystopia. Civil society, understood as organizations and interpersonal relationships unmediated by the state, does not exist. The destruction of institutions and relationships outside of state control provides the key feature of dystopian oppression.

Dystopian Themes: Freedom/Isolation/Hidden Evil

In his classic novel *The Brothers Karamazov*, Dostoyevsky presents an allegorical story. Christ returns to Earth, arriving in Spain during "the most terrible time of the Inquisition." The people recognize him as the Messiah. He is taken into custody. The Grand Inquisitor comes to Jesus' cell and proceeds to explain the true nature of the world. The Inquisitor says that freedom is a burden, a source of misery: "nothing has ever been more insupportable for a man and a human society than freedom." In freedom, men are "weak, vicious, worthless and rebellious." Eventually humanity says to its rulers, "make us your slaves, but feed us." The Inquisitor says that people love those who oppress them. They also love those who provide their material needs, since those are all that really exist. Rulers soothe the consciences of the masses, telling them that salvation awaits those who submit. The Grand Inquisitor says: "who can rule men if not he who holds their conscience and their bread in his hands?" (Dostoyevsky 1993: 25, 26, 31). The rulers, who know the real truth of existence (in this case, that the Devil really rules the world and there is no true salvation), take the burden of freedom (and thus responsibility) from the people. They take up the heavy yoke of authority despite its cost to their happiness. They "guard the mystery" protecting the great mass of people from the true terror of the world. Of course, the Grand Inquisitor's justifications are lies. They conceal a desire for earthly power. The Inquisitor's pose, as a man who has given up personal happiness so that others may live in peaceful ignorance, is a pretense based on a literal deal with the Devil. The pursuit of power for its own sake leads to the abyss.

"Grand Inquisitor" moments appear over and over again in dystopian works. A member of the ruling elite takes it upon himself (and it is almost always a man) to explain the "why" of a particular society. These justifications are almost always self-serving and false. As Krishan Kumar says: "take almost any anti-utopia written after the end of the nineteenth century and the strong chances are it will bear the imprint of the 'Legend of the Grand Inquisitor'" (1987: 122).

Forster's "The Machine Stops" describes a world in which human beings live in isolation from one another in rooms beneath the earth. They communicate solely by screens and find physical contact repellent. A single controlling device called "The Machine" guides their lives, providing light, heat, air, food and communications. The Machine continually monitors those who live inside it and mediates their interactions. Those who challenge the Machine are condemned as "unmechanical" and expelled to the supposedly dead surface of the Earth. Under its control, people have become physically weak. One character tries to exercise by holding his pillow out at arm's length for "minutes at a time." In an inversion of Spartan practice, the Machine destroys any infant "who promised undue strength." The inmates of the Machine have a "terror of direct experience" that causes them to avoid their fellow human beings and the natural world. Humanity produces nothing but "ideas" that, in reality, are merely the digested opinions of previous generations. Over time the Machine begins to decay. Its inhabitants, who have come to worship it, passively accept its decline. Eventually, the Machine fails, resulting in the death of all those who live within it. But hope for humanity remains, since some of those expelled from the Machine survive on the surface (Forster 1909).

According to its author, the story was "a critique of a dehumanized machine civilization, and what was seen as its corollary, the Wellesian World State" (Kumar 1987: 205). Forster resists the "standardizing, rationalizing, debilitating" world promised by technological progress (Moylan 2000: xii). Here we see another part of dystopian critique, the fear that, as technology advances, humanity becomes more and dependent, to the point where people cannot survive. The Machine might be considered a form of artificial intelligence designed to make our lives easier. We are warned that, in the end, technology will enslave and destroy humanity.

Le Guin's short story "The Ones Who Walk Away from Omelas" also presents key dystopian themes. The apparently utopian conditions of the city of Omelas are (ostensibly) maintained by the horrific oppression of a single child, who is kept locked in a room, deprived of all human contact and covered in its own filth. The child eventually goes mad. The members of this community are required to see this child, so they cannot claim ignorance. They are told that, if the child is freed, the utopia of Omelas will end. A few of those who are repulsed by the evil at the heart of the perfect community leave it. Those who "walk away" might be considered brave individuals heading out into the unknown, rejecting the injustice that sustained their old life. But those who walk away refuse to take responsibility for the evil actions of their community, since they fail to free the child held in such terrible conditions and face the consequences. In this case, "exit" is a sort of moral abdication. But there might be an even worse outcome. Most citizens come to justify the situation to themselves. Le Guin says: "their tears at the bitter injustice dry when they begin to perceive the terrible injustice of reality, and to accept it" (2004: 283). She also notes that those who stay are driven to perform noble acts and to work with greater commitment for the good of the community. "Omelas" is an obvious allegory of our own society. We live on the unseen exploitation of others. We devise theories to justify the oppression faced by most of the human race. We work to hide the evils of our world from ourselves. Dystopian works ask what we might do in the face of evil. The answers they provide are not comforting.

Zamyatin's Machine State

Zamyatin's *We* could be considered the first modern dystopian novel. He described it "as a warning against the two-fold danger which threatens humanity: the hypertrophic power of the machines and the hypertrophic power of the State" (quoted in Kumar 1987: 229). He addresses the dangers of leader worship and the enforced mechanization of society. In the "OneState," the assembly line industrial efficacy principles of Fredrick Winslow Taylor, later elevated to a quasi-religion by Henry Ford (and parodied by Huxley in *Brave New World*), are bought to their ultimate fruition. A leader (ironically) called the "Benefactor" rules over this regimented society. Elected yearly on the "Day of Unanimity," he bears a close resemblance to Lenin. In a nod to Plato's *Republic*, the OneState's secret police are called the "Bureau of Guardians." A numerical "Table" based on an ancient railroad timetable organizes the daily lives of the people. Zamyatin's satire is clear. But the work moves beyond satire.

The people of the OneState are identified by numbers and live in glass towers open to the gaze of all. As in many dystopias that follow, they have no families and, while they have complete sexual access to every other person, any experience of love or close personal connection is expressly forbidden. They are under total surveillance and are totally isolated. Every day, they march in ranks down the streets. The narrator, a disaffected engineer called D-503, relates the scene: "the numbers were marching along in step in neat ranks of four – hundreds and thousands of them in their sky-blue yunies with the golden badge on each chest bearing each one's state number." In the course of the narrative, D-503 becomes alienated from the state and is recruited by a rebel group. In the end, he is restored to loyalty through the removal of his "former illness (soul)" (Zamyatin 1993: 7, 224).

The OneState of *We* defines imagination as a disease and prescribes a "Great Operation" to remove it from the brain. This event is hailed as a great liberating moment for humanity. The state declares imagination "the last barrier on the path to happiness." Once it is removed, humans are "the equal to the machine," since they too will now act in a "precise and invariable rhythm, like that of the pendulum." After the Operation, citizens are "not men but some kind of tractors in human form" (Zamyatin 1993: 172, 173, 182). What Plato tried to achieve through education and myth-making, a community of total commitment and unity, the Benefactor achieves through a perverse application of science.

We has a Grand Inquisitor moment. D-503 faces the Benefactor, who explains that the OneState provides humanity with the greatest gift of all: "What is it that people beg for, dream about, torment themselves for, from the time they leave swaddling clothes? They want someone to tell them, once and for all, what happiness is – and then bind them to that happiness with a chain" (Zamyatin 1993: 207). Freedom is a burden fraught with worry. Here we understand the true meaning of the name "Benefactor." Like the Grand Inquisitor, or Plato's philosopher kings, he frees us from the burdens of choice and free will.

Huxley and Inhuman Stability

Huxley's *Brave New World* critiques the quasi-religious early twentieth-century vision of progress as an unalloyed good. He employs satire, engaging in word play reminiscent of More in *Utopia*. The names of the characters reference famous political, economic and cultural figures of the era. In what might be the most amusing example, the inhabitants of his World State (a direct reference to H. G. Wells) worship Henry Ford, whose autobiography functions as the bible and whose sayings represent the height of wisdom. This should not surprise us in a world where people's bodies and psyches are produced on an assembly line. The rulers of the World State have "assume[d] control over evolution" (Claeys 2017: 361). They have achieved, in a way meant to be horrifying, eugenic goals that appear in utopian thought as far back as Plato. The ruling caste, the Alphas, are almost genetically perfect (and emotionally empty).

As in *We*, the constructs of the World State (most of whom hardly qualify as people) are at once totally isolated and totally surveilled. A desire to be alone is seen as antisocial and a sign of serious mental imbalance. These individuals have no families and no intimate personal connections. They engage in state-mandated (heterosexual) promiscuity and use a narcotic drug (soma) when they feel lonely, sad or in any way out of sorts. All their physical needs are met. Their work is pleasant and fulfilling, since they are designed for the tasks they perform (Huxley 1998: 16, chap. 3). It might be possible to see *Brave New World* as a hedonistic utopia. But to do so would require accepting the treatment of human beings as pure mechanistic constructs, as objects, not as self-directing subjects.

The constructs of the World State ignore the past, both their society's and their own. They "live in an eternal present, with no idea of future or past" (Kumar 1987: 259). To look back on one's own life is considered to be a monumental breach of good taste. They quote Ford's maxim that "history is bunk." Cut off from past and future, they have no points of reference to challenge the existing order. When some of the characters attempt a pathetic rebellion, they lack any means to explain what they want, what change they desire (Huxley 1998: 212–16).

Huxley provides his version of the Grand Inquisitor moment when Mustapha Mond, the "World Controller," explains the nature of the World State. He says that "every change is a menace to stability." The World State's goals, "community, identity, stability," can only be maintained through the limitation of any form of free thought or inquiry. Mond says that "truth is a menace, science is public danger" (1998: 224, 227). Mond poses as a suffering servant who surrendered his true love, pure science, to assure the happiness of humanity, which he defines in purely material terms. He says "people are happy; they get what they want; and they never want what they can't get. They're well off; they're safe; they're never ill." Defining freedom in any other way can lead only to destruction. Mond says that, in the past, "people went on talking about truth and beauty as though they were sovereign goods ... What's the point of truth and beauty when the anthrax bombs are popping around you?" (1998: 220, 228). The people of the World State, like the inhabitants of many utopias, have traded freedom for security. Huxley suggests that this trade-off includes all that makes us truly human, including "the freedom to be unhappy, to express passion, spontaneity, and real joy" (Claeys 2017: 363).

Orwell and the Nihilism of Power

Orwell's *Nineteen Eighty-Four* confronts the dangerous growth of state power, the use and abuse of ideology, the application of propaganda as a conditioning tool, the surrender of liberty and, finally, the collapse of all political life into a pursuit of power for its own sake. Orwell clearly targets Stalinism, but he also points to the universal militarization and regimentation of society and the equally universal accumulation of power in the hands of the state. Orwell posits an acceleration or enhancement of existing conditions and trends. There are a number of satirical elements in the book. Big Brother is clearly mean to be Stalin, and Goldstein, the immortal enemy of Oceania, stands in for Leon Trotsky, the disgraced hero of the Soviet Revolution.

Objective reality does not exist in Oceania. The Party claims that "reality is inside the skull" and that all aspects of existence are under its control; 2 + 2 = 5 becomes a plausible statement in this situation, since reality is what the Party says it is. The Party rewrites the language, creating Newspeak, a debased form of English designed to make it impossible for people to express any complex or oppositional thought. There are no longer any laws, only the power of the Party. The Party continually rewrites history. The inhabitants of Oceania cannot be sure of the year or of the reality of the war continually waged by the state. The main character, Winston Smith, notes that "he did not know with any certainty whether this was 1984" (Orwell 1984: 162). His lover Julia, who is perhaps the most perceptive character in the book regarding the regime, suggests that Oceania launches rockets against its own people to maintain support for the war. In an echo of the Spartan practice of killing any Helots deemed to pose a threat, the Party eliminates any member of the despised working class, the "proles," who "were judged capable of being dangerous" (1984: 218). The true war is the war of the Party against the people.

In Oceania all bonds between individuals are severed. "No one dares trust a wife or a child or friend any longer." While people live in isolation, they are also under total surveillance and required to engage in mandatory group activities. Smith says: "In principle a Party member had no spare time ... when he was not working, eating, or sleeping he would be taking part in some communal recreation; to do anything that suggested a taste for solitude ... was always slightly dangerous." This "Ownlife" was evidence of criminal individuality. As its ultimate goal, the party seeks to create a world where "there will be no wives and no friends." In the future "there will be no loyalty, except loyalty to the Party. There will be no love, except the love of Big Brother" (Orwell 1984: 389, 227).

Nineteen Eighty-Four features a famous Grand Inquisitor moment. Smith is arrested and tortured by the Party leader O'Brien. O'Brien explains the goal and purpose of the Party as the simple pursuit of power. The Party and its functionaries have no higher goals, no great and noble purpose. They are not suffering servants who give up happiness for the common good. They simply seek to exercise domination over others. They are the "priests of power" in a world where "God is power." As Claeys observes, "the final portrayal of O'Brien reveals the intoxicating, self-deluding madness which absolute power induces" (2017: 421). O'Brien paints a picture of total nihilism. He says the Party is building a world where the only pleasure will be forcing your will upon someone else and making them suffer. "All competing pleasures will be destroyed. But always – do not forget this, Winston – always there will be the intoxication of power, constantly increasing and constantly growing subtler." O'Brien concludes with the well-known statement: "If you want a picture of the future, imagine a boot stamping on a human face – forever" (Orwell 1984: 386, 390). Since "freedom is slavery," the choice to submit to the Party becomes the only possible (perverted) expression of freedom. No attack on the Party's principles is possible, since the Party has no history, recognizes no law, and has no goals beyond power.

Atwood and Dystopian Isolation

In *The Handmaid's Tale*, the supposedly fundamentalist Christian state of Gilead controls a portion of the former United States. Like other dystopias, *The Handmaid's Tale* includes elements of satire. It appears to be set in Boston. The Puritans who founded Boston sought to build a theocratic utopian "city on a hill" as a model to the world. Several events in the book seem to occur on the campus of Harvard University.

Like Oceania, Gilead is at perpetual war with its own people. The regime relies on surveillance and acts of terror. Racial minorities have lost all rights, and all people who are not members the official Christian sect are enemies of the state subjected to genocidal violence. (Atwood is constructively vague about just what religious orthodoxy means in Gilead.) Women are the particular objects of Gilead's oppression. They are not allowed to write. They are taught that the "pen is envy." The Handmaids are women enslaved by the ruling elite for breeding purposes. Other women fear and hate the Handmaids. Under constant observation, they are isolated from one another and from the larger society. Signifying her position as a piece of property, the main character is called Offred. Cut off from all reference points, Offred desperately struggles to remember who she really is, her true self, her true name. She cannot be sure of the year or how long the regime has lasted. Offred finds it increasingly difficult to remember the past. What Orwell called the "locked loneliness" of isolation bears down on her. She says: "Things change so quickly, buildings can be torn down or turned into something else, it's hard to keep straight in your mind the way they used to be." She is told, chillingly, that future Handmaids will find their task easier. "They will accept their duties with willing hearts ... Because they won't want things they can't have" (Atwood 1998: 165, 117). The ruling elite and their servants, women called "Aunts" who are co-opted by the state to train and monitor the Handmaids, defend their actions as necessary for (white) racial survival. They also claim that they have liberated society from the false conception of freedom as the exercise of choice and acceptance of responsibility. An Aunt says: "There is more than one kind of freedom ... freedom from and freedom to. In the days of anarchy, it was freedom to. Now you are given freedom from. Don't underrate it." Gilead claims to have liberated women from the dangers posed by male violence (1998: 24). But as in *Nineteen Eighty-Four*, freedom for women in Gilead is indeed slavery.

In the book's Grand Inquisitor moment, Offred's owner (called the "Commander") attempts to justify Gilead. He lacks the bold, almost light-hearted self-assurance of Mustapha Mond or the insane but powerful confidence of O'Brien. Like many of the functionaries of the Nazi regime who carried out the Holocaust, he is a colorless bureaucrat. He seems almost pathetic in his desire to have Offred agree that what Gilead has done is right: "We thought we could do better." Offred wonders: "How can he think this is better?" His chilling response sums up the dystopian horror of ideologically driven political action. "Better never means better for everyone ... It always means worse, for some" (Atwood 1998: 211). Like the Grand Inquisitor, the Benefactor, Mond and O'Brien, the Commander defines freedom as liberation from the need to make choices.

The regime described by Atwood seems completely plausible. Each of the features of Gilead has been supported by notable political figures across the world in the last few decades. Governments enslave populations based on some essential characteristic, engage in ethnic cleansing, and murder the adherents of disfavored religions. Women's rights have been more and more constrained in the name of religion. "Dominionism," the belief that only Christians should have political rights, has many adherents in the United States.

Does dystopia provide any hope? Or was Kumar right when he said that, in major dystopian works, "the future was portrayed as a totalitarian hell in which all hope was extinguished and all exits closed?" (1987: 225). Zamyatin leaves the reader in an ambiguous position, as his hero is subdued by the OneState while the revolution against it seems to continue. Huxley shows the absurdity of revolution in his World State. While Orwell suggests that Oceania eventually falls and Atwood explicitly says Gilead fails, these hopes are not central to the works, since the main characters' efforts at resistance appear futile. (Atwood's sequel to *The Handmaid's Tale*, *The Testaments* (2019), set fifteen years after the events of the first novel, expands on the inner workings of Gilead and in doing so reflects on contemporary oppression and resistance. It is interesting to note that the film (1990) and television series (2017) based on the original book take a more hopeful position on the possibilities of resistance to the dystopian regime.)

The Dystopian Post-human

The end of contemporary humanity and its replacement with the superhuman or the post-human is a recurrent theme in dystopia. The film *Blade Runner* (1982) famously questioned the future of humanity when we create creatures "more human than human," while *Gattaca* (1997) presented a world where genetically imperfect humans were second-class citizens. In the video game series *BioShock* (2007 and 2010), a libertarian society is destroyed by conflicts over the distribution and use of genetic enhancements. We are attracted to the idea of an escape from the mundane limits imposed by our humanity. We should ask whether concern for the status of the individual is an artifact of modernity and whether this concern has become quaint in the face of biotechnology and the cyborg.

In *Oryx and Crake* (2003), Atwood makes a powerful statement about the possibilities of the post-human in a world destroyed by humanity. The title character Crake designs a new race of beings that look human but have none of the dangerously aggressive, individualistic traits of *Homo sapiens*. They are impervious to most disease and simply drop dead at thirty. They are beautiful but effectively non-sexual, mating only once a year, and have no capacity for sexual jealousy (2003: 302–6). In effect, the "Crakers" are not individuals in any real sense. Although they are given names, they lack any means to express political or social ideas beyond that of the herd. The "Crakers" are super-human and less than human at the same time.

The Crakers can be compared to the Alphas of *Brave New World*. Both are genetically engineered to fit within a particular social/ecological niche. They are not individuals, the Crakers by their design and the Alphas through condi-tioning. They are beautiful but vacant. Both Atwood and Huxley warn us of the seductive dangers of the post-human. They warn us that the sacrifices inherent in the creation of post-humans, such as the death of the vast majority of humanity in *Oryx and Crake* or the creation of human machines in *Brave New World*, may be too much to bear.

The Anthropocene as Dystopia

In the last few centuries human activity has become the dominant influence on the global environment. In this era, known as the Anthropocene, we have changed the planet to suit our needs at an irrevocable cost to the plants and animals with which we share it. Perhaps the most dystopian tendency in contemporary times can be found in discussions of the global environment and humanity's place in it. Are human beings a sort of plague, "a planetary disease organism," destroying the fabric of the world? (Lovelock 2010: 28). The idea that humans are a blight on the planet was forcefully expressed in the film *The Day the Earth Stood Still* (2008), in which the alien Klaatu says to a human, "If the Earth dies, you die. If you die the Earth survives." Another exchange between Klaatu and his human protector drives the point home. He says: "The human race is killing the earth. The problem is you." The human responds, in wonder and fear, "You came to save the earth from us."

It seems more and more certain that human beings and modern technological civilization have killed real, wild and untrammeled nature. "We have built a greenhouse, a *human creation*, where once there bloomed a sweet and wild garden" (McKibben 1990: 91, original emphasis). As John

Gray notes, "in wrecking the planetary environment humans are only doing what they have done innumerable times before on a local level" (2007: 209). Can "humans make it through what many scientists call this planet's latest great extinction – make it through and bring the rest of Life with us rather than tearing it down[?]" (Weisman 2007: 269). Can we survive climate change and all that follows?

The emerging environmental sensibility of the 1960s and 1970s made humanity more aware of the fragility of life and reflected concerns that humanity and nature were on a collision course. Films such as *Silent Running* (1972) and *Soylent Green* (1973) present visions of an earth overrun by humanity, stripped of all plant and animal life, and facing the end of all things. In *The Dispossessed* (1974), Ursula K. Le Guin presents a picture of an Earth murdered by humanity. Earth has become a planet where a few survivors struggle to keep the species alive in a wasteland (2011: 347–8).

The literary (and film) genre known as "cli-fi" (climate fiction) addresses human reactions to climate change. Works such as Marge Piercy's *He, She, and It* (1991), Octavia Butler's *Parable of the Sower* (1993) and, more recently, Omar El-Akkad's *American War* (2017) examine how environmental crisis combines with political, social and economic crisis to produce new and oppressive regimes. Like Atwood's Gilead, these regimes focus their violence on women and ethnic and racial minorities. *Blade Runner* (1982), Cormac McCarthy's *The Road* (book 2006, film 2009), *Wall-E* (2008) and *Elysium* (2013) examine the dystopian possibilities of the complete death of nature. *Blade Runner*'s replicants and artificial animals point to a post-human future of manufactured "life." McCarthy sees humanity's end as a cannibalistic nightmare in the ashes of a burned, dead planet. In *Wall-E*, humans have fled a desolate earth to live in space and have become physically weak and machine reliant, mirroring the people in "The Machine Stops." In *Elysium*, the wealthy live on a luxurious space station far above the poor, who are trapped on a ruined Earth.

An extreme and permanent separation of rich and poor is a staple of dystopian literature and film. In the distant future of H. G. Wells's *The Time Machine* (1895), the descendants of the ruling classes live above ground and have become childlike and vacant, while the descendants of the working classes live below ground and have become brutal, preying on their former masters for food. In the classic silent film *Metropolis* (1927), the decadent ruling class lives in the sunshine at the top of giant skyscrapers while the dehumanized working class lives below ground, serving machines. This theme is also seen in the *Hunger Games* (2008–15) series of books and films.

Recent non-fiction works on climate change proclaim the coming end of humanity. We are told we face "the end of normal; never normal again. We have already exited the state of environmental conditions that allowed the human animal to evolve in the first place" (Wallace-Wells 2019: 18). Our actions have created a wave of animal extinctions that might just end with our own (Kolbert 2014). In *The Revenge of Gaia* (2006), the English environmental scientist James Lovelock paints an apocalyptic picture of our future. Global climate change combined with our teeming numbers leave us with no escape. "It would be easy to think of ourselves and our families as incarcerated in a planet-sized condemned cell – a cosmic death row – awaiting inevitable execution." We face a situation where at best a few humans will survive in a world of deserts and howling wastes. "Before this century is over, billions of us will die and the few breeding pairs of people that survive will be in the arctic region where the climate remains tolerable." We are on "a rocky path to a new Stone Age existence on an ailing planet, one where few of us survive among the wreckage of our once biodiverse Earth." The last humans will be an "impoverished few survivors in a torrid society ruled by warlords on a hostile and disabled planet" (2006: 151, 154).

The Necessity of Dystopian Political Thought

Dystopia occupies an unusual place in utopian political thought. It is a warning against the dangers of utopian dreaming. It also awakens us to trends in our own times that promise to destroy what makes us human. Claeys says that we have lost control of our destiny to "elites, machines and systems," that we accept "monstrosity" and that "dystopia increasingly defines the spirit of our times." But he goes on to note that dystopian thought can "envision rational and collective solutions where irrationality and panic loom" (2017: 498, 501). It seems that the task of dystopian thought, whether as literature or film, or in more academic forms of speculation, is fearlessly to confront crisis and to delineate the dangers we face. We can only hope that the next steps, action to avert disaster and tyranny, remain possible.

8
Does Utopia Have a Future?

We live in what seem to be anti-utopian times. Frontiers, even the high frontier of space, seem to have been closed. Technology appears on the cusp of making humanity obsolete. Fashionable despair rules the intellectual horizon. Youth are repeatedly told that their lives will be less rich, less meaningful than those of their parents. Fears of the end of human civilization are part of our daily discourse. We face devastating climate change, economic collapse, nuclear war, or any number of other possible dooms. But when did we believe differently? Times of true utopian optimism are few and far between and generally short-lived. Whether it is the Enlightenment's "best of all possible worlds," the promise of human liberation through technology, or the promised end of political strife though universal peace, all such periods seem to come to a crashing and crushing end. When Francis Fukuyama (1989) proclaimed the "End of History" at the close of the Cold War, he declared that utopia had been achieved. He claimed liberal democracy and capitalism represented the end state of human development. But those dreams were revealed to be false.

Slavoj Žižek sees a failure of imagination at the heart of our current crisis. "Popular imagination is persecuted by the visions of the forthcoming 'breakdown of nature,' of the stoppage of all life on earth – it seems easier to imagine the 'end of the world' than a far more modest change in the mode of production" (quoted in Wegner 2014: 89). Fredric Jameson (2016) believes that utopian thought, faced with the triumph of "late capitalism," has been left voiceless, unable to articulate a coherent challenge to the oppression and despair of the present. Our malaise goes deep. In our current age, it has become fashionable to declare that progress is a lie, democracy a sham and human liberty an impossible dream. Authoritarian populism is resurgent. "Realists" denigrate utopian dreaming in favor of a hard-headed (in their view) vision of a world in which power defines justice. Reaction seems in full flight. Reason and science seem to have been rejected. We see the return of magical thinking and the re-creation of an enchanted world. Utopia has become identified with impossible dreams. Dystopian visions dominate our popular entertainment as zombies roam a desolate planet and children hunt each other for the entertainment of decadent elites.

Proclamations of the death of utopia occur with regular frequency. Jameson suggests that utopia's end can be seen in the current economic division of the world. In the impoverished half of the world, in the face of "misery, poverty, unemployment, starvation, squalor, violence and death ... the intricately elaborated social schemes of utopian thinkers become as frivolous as they are irrelevant." Meanwhile, in the rich half of the world "unparalleled wealth, computerized production, scientific and medical discoveries ... seem to have rendered utopian fantasy and speculation as boring and antiquated as pre-technological narratives of space flight" (2004: 35).

But while Jameson delineates the decline of utopia, he also notes its absolute necessity. He says: "it is difficult enough to imagine any radical political programme today without the conception of systemic otherness, of an alternate society, which only the idea of utopia seems to keep alive" (2004: 36). As Krishan Kumar says, "Utopian conceptions are indispensable to politics, and to progress; without them politics is a soulless void, a mere instrumentality without purpose or vision" (1991: 95). Utopian thought is vitally necessary to any healthy community. People must be allowed and, more importantly, allow themselves to dream, to launch their thought beyond what is socially expected and rewarded. If utopia is dead or meaningless, what is left of human aspiration? Utopian thought does not require some simple-minded concept of inevitable and unstoppable progress. But without utopian dreaming nothing new can be accomplished.

The Status of Utopia

Two of the "faces" of utopia identified by Lyman Tower Sargent (1994), utopian/dystopian fiction and intentional communities, seem to be in the throes of a renaissance. Utopian science fiction, often focused on ecological themes, finds a growing audience. For example, Kim Stanley Robinson's numerous novels, in particular the *Pacific Edge* series and his "Science in the Capitol" (2004–7) trilogy on climate change, seriously consider the possibilities of ecological utopianism. The genre of young adult (Y/A) dystopia provides utopian hope. Exemplified by Lois Lowry's *The Giver* (1993) and the *Hunger Games* (2008–10) series and its many imitators, Y/A dystopia points the way to a better future. In these books and films, heroic action overthrows evil regimes. Previously passive and atomized individuals join together and work for change. Mobilized people challenge the vision of the future as "a boot stamping on a human face, forever." Brave youths defeat oppression in almost every Y/A book and film. It is no accident that much contemporary utopian or dystopian literature is directed at the young adult market. Perhaps only young people retain enough optimism to hope for better things. The rise in youth activism demanding action on climate change represents one of the most hopeful signs of resurgent utopian dreaming, thought and action. But there is a dark side to the dystopian boom. Sometimes hope is twisted into the victory of some far-right band over "perceived communist, feminist, Islamist, liberal or socialist enemy, often with no distinction between the five" (Sargent 2017: 35). Such works dream of "utopias" for white Christians based on the destruction of the existing society in a cleansing wave of apocalyptic violence (Davis 1998: 330–8; Fitting 1991: 103–5).

Alienation and hyper-individualism characterized the twentieth century in the West. These conditions brought forward demands for the restoration of truly human values through new forms of communal experiments. Such communities ask if people can build a life outside or in opposition to the corrosive forces of global capitalism. Varieties of utopian dreaming can be seen in the small communities of religiously committed people, in cooperatives of many different kinds, in the growing number of consciously "green" intentional communities, and in any number of ideological or lifestyle enclaves and virtual communities (see Firth 2012; Cooper 2014; Sargisson 2012). Libertarians plan "seasteads" (intentional communities on the ocean) outside the reach of existing states (Quirk 2017). Utopia most often shows itself today in small communities of choice. It might be in these small experiments where the concrete utopia demanded by Ernst Bloch will manifest itself. But these types of communities, whether based in religious attachment or simply in shared interests, produce their own problems. How do such communities, these "everyday utopias" (Cooper 2014), face the larger world? Is this a sort of privatization of utopia, a declaration that large-scale utopian dreaming and change appear impossible? Are they merely lifeboats in which to try to escape a coming flood?

Unless the small scale becomes a base to change the larger society, it might become a sort of relic, an enclave of frozen time, frozen ideas and frozen practices such as the Amish, some of the surviving communes of the 1960s, or survivalists and religiously committed people hoping to restore the patriarchal values of the 1950s. The idea that we can wall ourselves off from the world can be a dangerous myth. While it might have been viable in past centuries when a frontier existed, such a mindset today represents a moral abdication that all too often leads to self-satisfaction and exclusion. As China Miéville says, "utopia can be toxic." The genocidal visions of survivalist groups such as the III Percenters in the United States seem to support this assessment. But we must reject the idea that all utopian dreaming leads to violence, oppression and totalitarianism. Otherwise the battle is lost before it begins.

The status of Sargent's "third face," utopian social/political thought, is more ambiguous. The academic study of utopia has boomed over the last fifty years. Scholars across many disciplines examine utopian justice, the role of intentional communities in political change, and the place of utopian dreaming in an age of climate change and global capital. But the academic study of utopia faces a set of hard questions about how to translate its insights into political action (see Johnson 2019). Ruth Levitas says: "The importance of utopian wishes hinges on the unfinished state of the material world. The world is in a constant state of process, of becoming. The future is 'not yet' and is a realm of possibility. Utopia reaches toward that future and anticipates it. And in doing so, it helps to effect the future" (1990: 14). To attain its full meaning, utopian thought must spur action.

The Future of Utopian Theory

To have meaning and power, contemporary utopian political thought must engage in an active defense of ideas of equality and common purpose. Thinking in utopian ways "enables each of us to become a whole person, an active citizen, empowered to join with each other in the collective work of deep social transformation" (Moylan 2018: 321). Utopian thought must "refer to institutions and practices that are by no means impossible but have not yet been brought into being" (Ingram 2016: xvii). In terms of actual political action, Erik Olin Wright (2010) suggests that any utopian project must focus on "social empowerment." By this he means citizen control over economic and political decision making, from the lowest to the highest level. He claims that a basic precondition of a real utopia must be a universal basic income. Such a guarantee will give citizens the freedom to take part in the management of their communities. Rutger Bregman suggests that "for the first time in history we are actually rich enough to finance a sizeable basic income" (2017: 43). The need for the security provided by a basic income for all will become clearer as even more of what we call work becomes the province of machines guided by artificial intelligence.

Utopian political thought must reject modest goals and end points. Utopian thought "is not oriented to what should be, but it is an exploration of what could be" (Bell 2017: 123). Our current crises force us to demand what seems impossible. After all, the once impossible has become possible often enough. The ideal of equality, of treating our fellow human beings as subjects worthy of respect and not as objects to be used, would have been understood as blasphemous madness for much of human history. (Such a position could be seen as a violation of the will of God or the gods, or as a violation of the immutable laws of nature.) A key principle of utopian political thought must remain making sure that no one can turn property (or money) into power. This might require small-scale communism or anarchist libertarianism with full exit, or it might require a form of radical democracy where most offices are filled by lottery. We must be open to radical speculation at all times. Like Plato, we must recognize that no existing society, and perhaps none we can currently imagine, fulfills all our expectations.

With these points in mind, consider these propositions as potential bases for contemporary utopian dreaming and action.

Five Propositions about Utopia

1 Utopia is necessary.
   We die without dreams of a better world. We are *Homo utopicus*.
2 Utopia has been realized.
   Millions of humans truly live like kings, or even gods.
3 Utopia is impossible.
   It has been tried, and it has failed, in horrible ways. Our very nature makes utopia impossible.
4 Utopia is dangerous.
   Utopia creates impossible desires. Utopia creates disappointment and nothing more. Utopia justifies bending the world out of shape to meet the demands of an ideology.
5 Utopia resists definition.
   But it can't mean just anything you want it to mean.

Five Propositions for Utopian Contemporary Political Thought

1   Utopian thought is humanist. Utopian thought is not utilitarian.

Any "utopian" vision that demands some (unwillingly) sacrifice to benefit others is wrong. Any vision that loves humanity but discounts the well-being and the very survival of human individuals cannot be utopian. Human beings cannot be treated as abstractions. They must be seen as individuals, each with unique value. In our times, no theory that treats people as mere cogs in a wheel or parts of a machine can be considered fully utopian.

2   Utopian thought is about liberation and unity (harmony).

Utopia seeks freedom from fear, from want, from arbitrary power, from the limits imposed on us by nature. It seeks to create communal unity and a society that works together for the common good. But attaining all of these goals, or even one of them, is inherently problematic, since freedom works against unity, and unity works against freedom. Utopia must allow citizens to voice demands for change and, if necessary, freely exit. A key challenge to any modern utopian theory remains how to encourage democracy and local control while avoiding the oppressive unity imposed by the tyranny of the majority and the potentially false harmony enforced by custom and norm.

3   Utopian thought is forward looking.

Utopian thought cannot merely be "retrotopian." There is no glorious golden age to re-create.

4   Utopian thought reshapes the limits of the possible.

Utopia lets us imagine a world that does not yet, and may never, exist. But, in the very act of imagining a world, we open our minds to new things, to new hopes, and create a desire for a better, more just world.

5   Utopian thought is not the same as ideology.

Utopian thought must recognize the dangers of positing a final resting point for human political activity or human aspiration, or in trying to make the real, messy human world conform to pre-existing ideas.

What is to be done?

Utopian political thought must aim at human liberation. One hundred years ago H. G. Wells provided a set of clear guidelines for utopian thought and action. He said we must recognize that "the essential value of all such speculation lies in this assumption of emancipation, lies in the regard toward human freedom, in the undying interest of the human power of self-escape, the power to resist the causation of the past, and to evade, initiate, endeavour and overcome" (2005: 13). But utopian speculation is not limitless or ungrounded. We must understand that we cannot fully escape the past or the traditions and lifeways we inhabit and that the wholly self-creating (or re-created) individual is a dangerous myth. Our emancipation can occur only in the context of our liberation in concert with that of our fellow human beings. We may find in utopian political thought the means to free humanity from fear, want and all the other oppressions that limit our potential. Utopians must continually fight against the dystopian idea that one person's freedom requires the oppression of others.

So, we must ask the perennial question: "What is to be done?" A place for utopian thought exists as long as we live in a world where "some manage to turn their wealth into power over others ... [where] other people are told their needs are not important, and their lives have no intrinsic worth" (Graeber and Wengrow 2018). Thomas More saw these conditions in 1516, and they remain the core of utopian critique and aspiration. A place for utopian thought will also remain so long as we remain *Homo utopicus*, beings who, "generation by generation, elaborate, and strive to realize, without ever wholly succeeding," dreams and hopes for equality and unity (Quarta 1996: 163).

In *Looking Backward*, Edward Bellamy challenged us to see that "the golden age lies before us, not behind us." As Levitas says, "the task before us to is to build the Republic of Heaven. Utopia ... entails refusal, the refusal to accept that what is given is enough" (2013: 17). Utopian thought remains critical to our understanding of the world, because we must have hope. Utopian dreaming allows us to "imagine a future and be in it" (Björk 2017). We must believe that we can create a more just and better world. Otherwise, we have nothing truly human to strive for.

References

Anderson, Benedict (1991) *Imagined Communities*. London: Verso.

Aristotle (1996) *The Politics* and *The Constitution of Athens* (ed. S. Everson). Cambridge: Cambridge University Press.

Ashcroft, Bill (2017) *Utopianism in Postcolonial Literatures*. New York: Routledge.

Atwood, Margaret ([1985] 1998) *The Handmaid's Tale*. New York: Anchor Books.

Atwood, Margaret (2003) *Oryx and Crake*. New York: Anchor Books.

Atwood, Margaret (2019) *The Testaments*. New York: Nan A. Talese.

Bader, Ralf (2011) The Framework for Utopia, in R. Bader and J. Meadowcroft (eds), *The Cambridge Companion to Nozick's "Anarchy, State and Utopia"*. Cambridge: Cambridge University Press.

Bammer, Angelika (2015) *Partial Visions: Feminism and Utopianism in the 1970s*. Oxford: Peter Lang.

Bauman, Zygmunt (2017) *Retrotopia*. Cambridge: Polity.

Baumgartner, Frederic (1999) *Longing for the End: A History of Millennialism in Western Civilization*. New York: St Martin's Press.

Beaumont, Matthew (2004) Oscar Wilde's Concept of Utopia: "The Soul of Man under Socialism," *Utopian Studies* 15: 13–29.

Bell, David M. (2017) *Rethinking Utopia: Place, Power and Affect*. New York: Routledge.

Bellamy, Edward (1891) "News from Nowhere": William Morris's Idea of the Good Time Coming, *New Nation* 1(3): 47.

Bellamy, Edward (1897) *Equality*. New York: Appleton.

Bellamy, Edward ([1888] 2007) *Looking Backward: 2000–1887* (ed. M. Beaumont). Oxford: Oxford University Press.

Björk (2017) Future Forever, *Utopia*. One Little Indian Ltd/ Wellhart Ltd.

Bloch, Ernst ([1954–9] 1986) *The Principle of Hope* (trans. N. Plaice, S. Plaice and P. Knight). Oxford: Blackwell.

Boesky, Amy (1996) *Founding Fictions: Utopias in Early Modern England*. Athens: University of Georgia Press.

Bregman, Rutger (2017) *Utopia for Realists: How We Can Build the Ideal World*. New York: Little, Brown.

Callenbach, Ernest ([1975] 1990) *Ecotopia*. New York: Bantam Books.

Cartledge, Paul (2003) *The Spartans: The World of the Warrior-Heroes of Ancient Greece, from Utopia to Crisis to Collapse*. New York: Overlook Press.

Cave, A. A. (1991) Thomas More and the New World, *Albion* 23: 209–29.

Cavendish, Margaret (2003) *Political Writings* (ed. S. James). Cambridge: Cambridge University Press.

Claeys, Gregory (2011) *Searching for Utopia: The History of an Idea*. New York: Thames & Hudson.

Claeys, Gregory (2017) *Dystopia: A Natural History*. Oxford: Oxford University Press.

Claeys, Gregory (2018) *Marx and Marxism*. New York: Nation Books.

Claeys, Gregory, and Lyman Tower Sargent (2017) Preface, in Claeys and Sargent (eds), *The Utopia Reader*. New York: New York University Press.

Cooper, Davina (2014) *Everyday Utopias: The Conceptual Life of Promising Spaces*. Durham, NC: Duke University Press.

Davis, J. C. (1981) *Utopia and the Ideal Society: A Study of English Utopian Writing, 1516–1700*. Cambridge: Cambridge University Press.

Davis, Laurence (2005) The Dynamic and Revolutionary Utopia of Ursula K. Le Guin, in Davis and P. Stillman (eds), *The New Utopian Politics of Ursula K. Le Guin's "The Dispossessed"*. Lanham, MD: Lexington Books.

Davis, Mike (1998) *Ecology of Fear: Los Angeles and the Imagination of Disaster*. New York: Metropolitan Books.

Dawson, Doyne (1992) *Cities of the Gods: Communist Utopias in Greek Thought*. Oxford: Oxford University Press.

Dostoevsky, Fyodor ([1880] 1993) *The Grand Inquisitor: With Related Chapters from "The Brothers Karamazov"* (ed. C. Guignon, trans. C. Garnett). Indianapolis: Hackett.

Dutton, Jacqueline (2010) "Non-Western" Utopian Traditions, in G. Claeys (ed.): *The Cambridge Companion to Utopian Literature*. Cambridge: Cambridge University Press.

Ferguson, John (1975) *Utopias of the Classical World*. Ithaca, NY: Cornell University Press.

Finley, M. I. (1975) *The Use and Abuse of History*. New York: Viking Press.

Firth, Rhiannon (2012) *Utopian Politics: Citizenship and Practice*. New York: Routledge.

Fischbach, Franck (2016) Marx and Utopia, in S. D. Chrostowska and J. D. Ingram (eds), *Political Uses of Utopia: New Marxist, Anarchist, and Radical Democratic Perspectives*. New York: Columbia University Press.

Fitting, Peter (1991) Utopia beyond Our Ideals: The Dilemma of the Right-Wing Utopia, *Utopian Studies* 2: 95–109.

Forster, E. M. (1909) The Machine Stops, *Oxford and Cambridge Review*, November.

Fourier, Charles (1996) *The Theory of the Four Movements* (ed. G. S. Jones and I. Patterson). Cambridge: Cambridge University Press.

Fraistat, Shawn (2015) The Authority of Writing in Plato's *Laws*, *Political Theory* 43: 657–77.

Friedman, Milton ([1962] 1982) *Capitalism and Freedom*. Chicago: University of Chicago Press.

Fukuyama, Francis (1989) The End of History, *The National Interest* 16: 3–18.

Gandhi, Mahatma (1996) *Selected Political Writings* (ed. Dennis Dalton). Indianapolis: Hackett.

Geoghegan, Vincent (1987) *Utopianism and Marxism*. London: Methuen.

Gilman, Charlotte Perkins (1999) *The Yellow Wall-Paper, Herland, and Selected Writings*. New York: Penguin Classics.

Graeber, David, and David Wengrow (2018) How to Change the Course of Human History (at Least, the Part That's Already Happened). *Eurozine* 2 March, www.eurozine.com/change-course-human-history.

Gray, John (2007) *Black Mass: Apocalyptic Religion and the Death of Utopia*. New York: Farrar, Straus & Giroux.

Green, Peter (1990) *Alexander to Actium: The Historical Evolution of the Hellenistic Age*. Berkeley: University of California Press.

Hamilton, Alexander, James Madison and John Jay ([1787–8] 2003) *The Federalist with Letters of "Brutus"* (ed. T. Ball). Cambridge: Cambridge University Press.

Harrington, James ([1656] 1992) *The Commonwealth of Oceana* and *A System of Politics* (ed. J. G. A Pocock). Cambridge: Cambridge University Press.

Huxley, Aldous (1962) *Island*. New York: Harpers.

Huxley, Aldous ([1932] 1998) *Brave New World*. New York: HarperPerennial.

Ingram, James (2016) Introduction: Politics and Utopia, in S. D. Chrostowska and J. D. Ingram (eds), *Political Uses of Utopia: New Marxist, Anarchist and Radical Democratic Perspectives*. New York: Columbia University Press.

Jacoby, Russell (2005) *Picture Imperfect: Utopian Thought for an Anti-Utopian Age*. New York: Columbia University Press.

Jameson, Fredric (2004) The Politics of Utopia, *New Left Review* 25 (January–February): 35–51.

Jameson, Fredric (2016) *An American Utopia: Dual Power and the Universal Army*. London: Verso.

Johns, Alessa (2010) Feminism and Utopianism, in G. Claeys (ed.), *The Cambridge Companion to Utopian Literature*. Cambridge: Cambridge University Press.

Johnson, Bonnie (2019) The Party of Utopia: A Report from the 43rd Annual Society for Utopian Studies Conference, *Los Angeles Review of Books* May 15, https://lareviewofbooks. org/article/the-party-of-utopia-a-report-from-the-43rd-annual-society-for-utopian-studies-conference.

Kinna, Ruth (2011) Politics, Ideology and Utopia: A Defence of Eutopian Worlds, *Journal of Political Ideologies* 16: 279–94.

Kolbert, Elizabeth (2014) *The Sixth Extinction: An Unnatural History*. New York: Picador.

Kuhlmann, Hilke (2005) *Living Walden Two: B. F. Skinner's Behaviorist Utopia and Experimental Communities*. Urbana: University of Illinois Press.

Kumar, Krishan (1987) *Utopia and Anti-Utopia in Modern Times*. Oxford: Blackwell.

Kumar, Krishan (1991) *Utopianism*. Minneapolis: University of Minnesota Press.

Le Guin, Ursula K. ([1973] 2004) The Ones Who Walk Away from Omelas, in *The Wind's Twelve Quarters*. New York: HarperPerennial.

Le Guin, Ursula K. ([1974] 2011) *The Dispossessed*. New York: Harper Voyager.

Lepore, Jane (2017) A Golden Age for Dystopian Fiction, *New Yorker* June 5–12, www.newyorker.com/magazine/2017/06/05/a-golden-age-for-dystopian-fiction.

Levitas, Ruth (1990) Educated Hope: Ernst Bloch on Abstract and Concrete Utopia, *Utopian Studies* 1(2): 13–26.

Levitas, Ruth (2000) For Utopia: The (Limits of the) Utopian Function in Late Capitalist Society, *Critical Review of International Social and Political Philosophy* 3(2–3): 25–43.

Levitas, Ruth (2013) *Utopia as Method*. New York: Palgrave Macmillan.

Lovelock, James (2006) *The Revenge of Gaia: Earth's Climate Crisis and the End of Humanity*. New York: Basic Books.

Lovelock, James (2010) *The Vanishing Face of Gaia: A Final Warning*. New York: Basic Books.

Mannheim, Karl ([1936] 1991) *Ideology and Utopia: An Introduction to the Sociology of Knowledge* (trans. L. Wirth and E. Shils). London: Routledge.

Manuel, Frank (1966) Toward a Psychological History of Utopias, in F. Manuel (ed.), *Utopians and Utopian Thought*. Boston: Houghton Mifflin.

Marx, Karl (1994) *Early Political Writings* (ed. J. O'Malley). Cambridge: Cambridge University Press.

Marx, Karl (1996a) *Capital, Volume 1*, in K. Marx and F. Engels, *Collected Works, Volume 35*. New York: International.

Marx, Karl (1996b) *Later Political Writings* (ed. T. Carver). Cambridge: Cambridge University Press.

McCutcheon, Elizabeth (1969) Thomas More, Raphael Hythlodaeus, and the Angel Raphael, *Studies in English Literature 1500–1900* 9(1): 21–38.

McKibben, Bill (1990) *The End of Nature*. New York: Anchor Books.

More, Thomas ([1516] 1989) *Utopia* (ed. G. Logan and R. Adams). Cambridge: Cambridge University Press.

Morris, William (2004) *News from Nowhere and Other Writings* (ed. C. Wilmer). London: Penguin Classics.

Moylan, Tom (2000) *Scraps of the Untainted Sky: Science Fiction, Utopia, Dystopia*. Boulder, CO: Westview Press.

Moylan, Tom (2014) *Demand the Impossible: Science Fiction and the Utopian Imagination*. Oxford: Peter Lang.

Moylan, Tom (2018) Transgressive, Totalizing, Transformative: *Utopia's* Utopian Surplus, *Utopian Studies* 29: 309–24.

Nozick, Robert (1974) *Anarchy, State and Utopia*. New York: Basic Books.

Orwell, George ([1949] 1984) *Nineteen Eighty-Four* (ed. B. Crick). Oxford: Oxford University Press.

Owen, Robert ([1813] 2019) *A New View of Society*. Lagos: Origami Books.

Paine, Thomas (1969) *The Complete Writings of Thomas Paine* (ed. P. Foner). New York: Citadel Press.

Paine, Thomas (2000) *Political Writings* (ed. B. Kuklick). Cambridge: Cambridge University Press.

Parrington, John (2003) H. G. Wells's Eugenic Thinking of the 1930s and 1940s, *Utopian Studies* 14(1): 74–81.

Plato (1973) *Phaedrus* and *Letters VII and VIII* (trans. W. Hamilton). London: Penguin Classics.

Plato (2000) *The Republic* (ed. G. R. F. Ferrari, trans. T. Griffith). Cambridge: Cambridge University Press.

Plato (2016) *The Laws* (ed. M. Schofield, trans. T. Griffith). Cambridge: Cambridge University Press.

Plutarch (1988) *Plutarch on Sparta* (ed. and trans. R. Talbert). London: Penguin Classics.

Popper, Karl (2013) *The Open Society and its Enemies*. Princeton, NJ: Princeton University Press.

Quarta, Cosimo (1996) Homo Utopicus: On the Need for Utopia, *Utopian Studies* 7(2): 153–65.

Quirk, Joe (2017) *Seasteading*. New York: Free Press.

Ramiro Avilés, Miguel A. (2003) On Law and Utopia: A Reply to Shulamit Almog, *Utopian Studies* 14: 132–42.

Rawls, John (2001) *The Law of Peoples*. Cambridge, MA: Harvard University Press.

Rawson, Elizabeth (1969) *The Spartan Tradition in European Thought*. Oxford: Clarendon Press.

Ricoeur, Paul (1986) *Lectures on Ideology and Utopia* (ed. G. Taylor). New York: Columbia University Press.

Roberts, Dorothy (2009) Race, Gender, and Genetic Technologies: A New Reproductive Dystopia? *Signs* 34: 783–804.

Robertson, Michael (2018) *The Last Utopians: Four Late Nineteenth-Century Visionaries and Their Legacy*. Princeton, NJ: Princeton University Press.

Roochnik, David (2009) The Political Drama of Plato's Republic, in S. Salkever (ed.), *The Cambridge Companion to Ancient Greek Political Thought*. Cambridge: Cambridge University Press.

Rousseau, Jean-Jacques (1997a) *The Discourses and Other Early Political Writings* (ed. and trans. V. Gourevitch). Cambridge: Cambridge University Press.

Rousseau, Jean-Jacques (1997b) *The Social Contract and Other Later Political Writings* (ed. and trans. V. Gourevitch). Cambridge: Cambridge University Press.

Ryan, Alan (2012) *On Politics: A History of Political Thought*. New York: Liveright.

Sargent, Lyman Tower (1994) The Three Faces of Utopianism Revisited, *Utopian Studies* 5(1): 1–37.

Sargent, Lyman Tower (2006) In Defense of Utopia, *Diogenes* 53(1): 11–17.

Sargent, Lyman Tower (2008) Ideology and Utopia: Karl Mannheim and Paul Ricoeur, *Journal of Political Ideologies* 13: 263–73.

Sargent, Lyman Tower (2009) *Contemporary Political Ideologies: A Comparative Analysis*. Belmont, CA: Wadsworth, Cengage Learning.

Sargent, Lyman Tower (2010) *Utopianism: A Very Short Introduction*. Oxford: Oxford University Press.

Sargent, Lyman Tower (2013) Ideology and Utopia, in M. Freeden, L. T. Sargent and M. Stern (eds), *The Oxford Handbook of Political Ideologies*. Oxford: Oxford University Press.

Sargent, Lyman Tower (2017) Ideology and Utopia: Karl Mannheim and Paul Ricoeur, in Z. Czıganyik (ed.), *Utopian Horizons: Ideology, Politics and Literature*. Budapest: Central European University Press.

Sargisson, Lucy (1996) *Contemporary Feminist Utopianism*. New York: Routledge.

Sargisson, Lucy (2012) *Fool's Gold: Utopianism in the Twenty-First Century*. New York: Palgrave Macmillan.

Schaer, Ronald (2000) Some Utopian Aspects of the French Revolution, in Schaer, G. Claeys and L.T. Sargent (eds), *Utopia: The Search for the Ideal Society in the Western World*. Oxford: Oxford University Press.

Segal, Howard P. (2012) *Utopias: A Brief History from Ancient Writings to Virtual Communities*. Malden, MA: Wiley-Blackwell.

Siméon, Ophélie (2017) *Robert Owen's Experiment at New Lanark: From Paternalism to Socialism*. London: Palgrave Macmillan.

Skinner, B. F. ([1948] 2005) *Walden Two*. Indianapolis: Hackett.

Stillman, Peter (1990) Recent Studies in the History of Utopian Thought, *Utopian Studies*, 1: 103–10.

Strong, Tracy (1994) *Jean-Jacques Rousseau: The Political of the Ordinary*. Thousand Oaks, CA: Sage.

Talmon, J. L. (1985) *The Origins of Totalitarian Democracy*. Boulder, CO: Westview Press.

Taylor, Keith (1982) *The Political Ideas of the Utopian Socialists*. London: Frank Cass.

Thaler, Mathias (2018) Hope Abjuring Hope: On the Place of Utopia in Realist Political Theory, *Political Theory* 45: 671–97.

Wallace-Wells, David (2019) *The Uninhabitable Earth: Life after Warming*. New York: Tim Duggan Books.

Wegner, Philip (2014) *Shockwaves of Possibility: Essays on Science Fiction, Globalization and Utopia*. Oxford: Peter Lang.

Weisman, Alan (2007) *The World without Us*. New York: St Martin's Press.

Wells, H. G. (1923) *Men Like Gods*. New York: Macmillan.

Wells, H. G. ([1905] 2005) *A Modern Utopia* (ed. G. Claeys and P. Parrinder). London: Penguin Classics.

Wenner, Danielle (2017) The Need for Non-Ideal Theory: A Case Study in Deliberative Democracy, in M. Weber and K. Vallier (eds), *Political Utopias: Contemporary Debates*. Oxford: Oxford University Press.

Winstanley, Gerrard (1941) *The Works of Gerrard Winstanley* (ed. G. Sabine). Ithaca, NY: Cornell University Press.

Wolin, Sheldon (2004) *Politics and Vision: Continuity and Innovation in Western Political Thought*. Princeton, NJ: Princeton University Press.

Wollstonecraft, Mary ([1792] 1995) *A Vindication of the Rights of Men* and *A Vindication of the Rights of Woman* (ed. S. Tomaselli). Cambridge: Cambridge University Press.

Wright, Erik Olin (2010) *Envisioning Real Utopias*. London: Verso.

Xenophon (1988) Spartan Society, in R. Talbert (ed. and trans), *Plutarch on Sparta*. London: Penguin Classics.

Zamyatin, Yevgeny ([1924] 1993) *We* (trans. C. Brown). London: Penguin Classics.

Index